Status of Adivasis/Indigenous
Peoples Land Series – 7

ANDHRA PRADESH

DISCLAIMER

Status of Adivasis/Indigenous Peoples Land Series – 7

ANDHRA PRADESH

Palla Trinadha Rao

Status of Adivasis/Indigenous Peoples Land Series – 7 :
ANDHRA PRADESH

Palla Trinadha Rao

First Published, 2014

ISBN 978-93-5002-270-2

Published by
AAKAR BOOKS
28 E Pocket IV, Mayur Vihar Phase I, Delhi 110 091
Phone: 011 2279 5505 Telefax: 011 2279 5641
aakarbooks@gmail.com; www.aakarbooks.com

In association with
THE OTHER MEDIA
J 139, First Floor, Vikas Puri
New Delhi 110 018
Phones: 011 2854 3372/73, Fax: 011 4237 1129
Email: tom@theothermedia.org

Printed at
Saurabh Printers Pvt. Ltd., A 16, Sector IV, Noida

Acknowledgements

The Status of Adivasis/Indigenous Peoples (SAIP) has been an important initiative of The Other Media and All India Coordinating Forum of Adivasis/Indigenous Peoples. It began with a lot of interest and enthusiasm with a wide consultation among activists, scholars and researchers interested in Adivasis/Indigenous People's issues. However, the process seemed to have had its own pace and could not keep up with the expectation of completing the report on time. The present phase of the programme has covered, state-wise, issues of land and mining in the Adivasis/Indigenous People's areas.

This report on land issues in the Adivasi areas of Andhra Pradesh has been prepared by Palla Trinadha Rao. We gratefully acknowledge the efforts made by the author and members of the Editorial Collective (EC) in preparing this report.

Members of the EC went through the report and gave their valuable comments and suggestions. We gratefully acknowledge their contribution that was available at every stage of preparation of the report. The efforts of the EC have been untiringly coordinated by C R Bijoy. The reports owe a lot to his relentless efforts to keep in the loop everyone concerned towards producing good results out of the reports. At the level of The Other Media, Ravi Hemadri, who worked as the Executive Director of the organisation through most part of the programme serves as a link between the organisation and the EC. He continued to coordinate the final editing and printing of the reports. We gratefully acknowledge the role played by both C R Bijoy and Ravi Hemadri.

We acknowledge and thank the Adivasi Academy, Tejgarh, Gujarat, and particularly Prof Ganesh Devy, for generously hosting in February, 2008, a two-day workshop of members of the EC and authors to review the draft reports. We thank the members of the Advisory Board of the SAIP, who with their participation in the first consultation and later whenever called upon, gave their inputs to the reports. Thanks are due to Shankar Gopalakrishnan who meticulously put together statistical data and selected literature for SAIP.

Finally we would like to acknowledge and thank our funders ICCO, Netherlands, and TROCAIRE, Ireland, who supported the programme right through the last five years. We are grateful to the Foundation for Ecological Security, Anand, Gujarat, and OXFAM who generously supported the printing of the first phase of reports on land. We thank all of them for being patient with this initiative.

E Deenadayalan
General Secretary

Contents

List of Tables and Figures

Tables

Figures

Acronyms and Abbreviations

APCCR	Andhra Pradesh Communist Committee of Revolutionary
Art	Article
ALD	Andhra Legal Decisions
ALT	Andhra Law Times
AP	Andhra Pradesh
AIR	All India Reporter
CPI (M)	Communist Party of India (Marxist)
CPI (ML)	Communist Party of India (Marxist-Leninist)
E G Dist	East Godavari District
GO	Government Order
GoI	Government of India
Hec	Hectares
ITDA	Integrated Tribal Development Agency
LTRP	Land Transfer Regulation Petition
NA	Not Available
NGO	Non-Government Organisation
PESA	Panchayats (Extension to Scheduled Areas) Act, 1996
Ref. No	Reference Number
RSR	Resettlement Survey Register
SC	Scheduled Caste
SDC	Special Deputy Collector
Asst.	Assistant
SLP	Special Leave Petition

TAC	Tribal Advisory Council
VSS	Vana Samrakshana Samithi
WG Dist	West Godavari District
WP	Writ Petition

Glossary and Legal Terms

Abkari tax	Excise Tax.
Adangal	A revenue account which shows cultivation and pattadar details of land.
Adivasi	Original inhabitants/Aboriginal, member of Scheduled Tribe.
Agency areas	These are areas governed by the Agent to the Government during the British period for administration of both civil and criminal justice. The revenue officials are designated as Agent, Asst. Agent and Agency Munsif (in charge of a Taluk). The Scheduled Areas of Andhra Pradesh are also popularly called Agency Areas.
Agency Divisional Officer	An officer in charge of a Revenue division.
Agent to Government	Government official of the rank of District Collector is designated as Agent to Government, during the British period under AP Agency Rules 1924 for administration of civil justice in agency areas.
Assigned or D form patta lands	Lands which are assigned by the revenue officials to the landless eligible persons for enjoyment of government lands.
Asst. Agent to Government	A subordinate officer to the Agent to Government. The official rank of Revenue Divisional Officer/Sub-Collector is designated as Asst.

	Agent to Government for administration of civil justice.
Deshmukh	District revenue official.
De hors	Outside or beyond the bounds of.
Diwan	Supervisory staff of a landlord's estate or *jagir.*
Encroachment	Encroachment means the unauthorized occupation of government land.
Fasali	The revenue year commencing from the first of July to the end of June of the following year.
Fifth Schedule	Fifth Schedule of the Constitution of India pertains to the governance of Scheduled Areas.
Hill tribe	Anybody or class of persons resident in the Agency Tracts.
Ipso facto	By the fact itself.
Izara land	A lease or farm land held at a defined rent or revenue.
Karnam	Village level revenue official.
Kistu	Payment of revenue on instalment basis.
Land Tenure system	Arrangement made by the British administration to collect land revenue from the cultivators of the land.
Mahal	Unit of revenue assessment.
Mansabs	Feudal chieftain/a head man of village/watch and ward.
Mutta	A village or group of villages held by a *Muttadar.*
Muttadar	A person who holds *Mutta* under a Sanad granted by the government subject to payment of a fixed amount of land revenue and who assists the government in maintaining law and order in the *Mutta.*
Patta	Land entitlement deed.
Pattadar	The *Ryotwari* proprietor is usually termed as pattadar.
Per se	By or in itself or themselves; intrinsically
Plain area	Other than the Scheduled Area
Podu	Shifting cultivation or slash and burn cultivation.
Proprietor	Landlord or Landholder of villages held by Estate, *Mutta, Mukasa.*

Rampa country	The Agency Area of Rampa notified as Rampa country in June 1879 under the Scheduled Districts Act 1874 in Madras Presidency.
Res judicata	No court shall try any suit in which the matter between the same parties, litigating under the same title, was already tried and decided by the competent court. The earlier judgement operates as res judicata in subsequent suit.
Revenue Village	A local area which is designated as a village by the government in the revenue accounts for the purposes of revenue administration.
Ryot	Cultivators of land.
Sanad	An acknowledgement and documentary proof of rights conferred upon by the government.
Scheduled Areas	The Fifth Schedule under Art.244(1) of the Constitution defines "Scheduled Areas" as such areas that the President may by order declare to be Scheduled Areas after consultation with the Governor of that State.
Scheduled Districts	Districts notified by the British under Scheduled Districts Act 1874.
Scheduled Tribe	Any tribe or tribal community or part of or group within any tribe or tribal community and specified as such in relation to the State of Andhra Pradesh notified by the President of India under Article 342 of the Constitution of India.
SDC court	Special Deputy Collector (Tribal Welfare) is a designated enquiry officer under Land Transfer Regulations to conduct enquiries for restoration of lands from the possession of non-tribals in the Scheduled Areas. The court is manned by SDC.
Settled villages/ Government Villages/ Ryotwari	Villages which were surveyed and settled during the British period in the year 1902-05 and 1932-35. Ryotwari tenure means the lands which

	were not covered by Zamindari, Muttadari, Mokasadari, etc.
Settlement Patta	Land title issued by the Settlement Officer under Survey and Settlement Regulations under 2 of 69; 2 of 70, etc.
Shikmidar	Shareholder of landed property.
Suo moto cases	Cases identified and taken by the government on its own initiative.
Survey	Includes all operations incidental to the determination, measurement and record of a boundary and includes resurvey.
Survey Number	Land numbered by the Survey and Settlement Department of the Government.
Taluk	A geographical revenue unit; a number of taluks constitute a District.
Tenant	A person who holds on lease land belonging to another.
Unassessed waste land	Unassessed waste land is a land to which no classification and assessment have been assigned. It is one of the categories of land that are prima facie available for assignment.
Zamindar	Landlord/land owner.
Zamindari	Estate owned by Zamindar.

Preface

Eighty-eight million Adivasis and indigenous peoples live in India—approximately one-fourth of the world's total indigenous population. Historically self-sufficient, forest-based communities with independent cultural identities they have been subjected to displacement, dispossession and repression for more than a century and are now India's poorest and most marginalized communities. Since the onset of British rule, and in many cases from much earlier, Adivasis and indigenous peoples have been systematically and forcibly dispossessed of the resources of their homelands. In gross violation of democratic practice, social justice and both constitutional and legal requirements, such dispossession continues to this day. It is also the Adivasis and indigenous peoples who have paid the heaviest price for the current neo-liberal globalisation policies, with their land, resources and forests taken from them for private capital—in the name of 'economic growth'.

These larger processes have been accompanied by the erosion and undermining of cultural identities, leading to a loss of cultural moorings and other markers of ethnicity. Less than half of India's Adivasi communities speak their own language. State and private efforts at 'mainstreaming' and against indigenous faiths, practices and cultural mores have had a devastating impact.

Such trends have not gone unchallenged. Despite

growing differentiation, ethnicity has emerged as a strong, consolidating force. Many have organised, often with the help of sympathetic outsiders, to fight against their oppressors and struggle for the control over land and other resources, and for local self-government as in parts of Central India. There have been demands for political self-determination and autonomy of varying degrees as in Jharkhand and the north-east. The state characterises all such struggles as 'Law and Order Problems', and large parts of central India and the north-east are heavily militarised in the name of 'national security'. In other parts too state repression has been heavy and brutal.

Though these processes are well-known to many and particularly to Adivasis and indigenous people's movements, there continues to be a dearth of knowledge on the overall status of Adivasis and indigenous peoples in India. The struggle-based mass organisations of Adivasis and indigenous peoples in the Indian subcontinent articulated the need to work towards such a task in the late 1990s. The collective process to fulfil this task was launched in 2005.

The Status of Adivasis/Indigenous Peoples is conceptualised as a series of reports on salient themes affecting the lives of Adivasis/Indigenous Peoples. In the first instance, the series focuses on the situation of land and mining in the tribal tracts of the country. We hope that the series will be effective in not only deliberating upon similar themes of importance to the Adivasi present and future, but also help strengthening linkages amongst movements, activists, scholars and all others who are concerned with the protection of the rights of Adivasis/Indigenous Peoples in the Indian subcontinent.

This series of reports will explore the history, the laws, and the facts, and describe struggles while providing an overview of current realities. The main purpose of these reports is to expand linkages and relationships between movements, scholars, and activists so that the future of the political struggles is informed and forward looking.

Editorial Collective on The Status of Adivasis/Indigenous Peoples

Alex Ekka, Bela Bhatia, Bijaya Panda, Bijoy Daimari, C R Bijoy, E Deenadayalan, Ganesh Devy, Nandini Sundar, Pradip Prabhu, Ravi Hemadri, Shankar Gopalakrishnan

Members of the Advisory Board on the Status of Adivasis/ Indigenous Peoples

Agapit Tirkey, Artax Shimray, B D Sharma, Dino Dean Gracious, Gam Shimray, Gina Shangkham, Johannes Laping, Joseph Bara, Joseph Marianus Kujur, Kekhri Yhome, Luingam Luithui, M Kunhaman, Madhu Sarin, Nikunja Bhutia, Rahul Banerjee, Rakesh Kapoor, Ramdayal Munda, Sanjay Basu Mullick, Stan Lourdusamy, Sukhendu Debbarma, Sumanta Banerjee, Tado Karlo, Tiplut Nongbri, Virginius Xaxa

Author's Note

I sincerely thank the Editorial Collective of SAIP for bringing out study papers under the SAIP Land Series in the country to provide information to understand the situation across the subcontinent and sharpen the strategies for struggles of Adivasis. I am also thankful to them for their valuable comments on the study report. It is important to acknowledge, Laya, a non-government organisation based in Visakhapatnam for encouraging me to contribute to this land series. My special thanks to Prof M Gopinathreddy, Centre for Economics and Social Studies (CESS), Hyderabad, for his comments on the study report.

Palla Trinadha Rao

Executive Summary

Land tenure has been the major sensitive political issue in the Scheduled Area of the State. Agriculture is the main source of income and livelihood for the majority of tribal people. But large tracts of land are concentrated in the hands of predominantly elite non-tribal sections. Consequently the tribal people are marginalised and deprived of their traditional land rights. The alien systems of land tenures have had far-reaching adverse effects on the dignity of the tribal people and their access to justice.

The tribal people have a long and proud history. It includes a rich historical and cultural linkage with natural resources. This unwritten relationship, however, has been altered or even taken away upon the arrival of non-tribal settlers from plain areas. The introduction of various land-related laws and documentation alien to tribals and their territories, and the imposition of alien modes of governance began a cycle of land occupations by non-tribals, its legitimisation by land reforms policy and law, and finally the dispossession of tribal people of their control over land. Together with these is the loss of identity along with the helplessness from being oppressed, and rights ignored and violated. Tribal people's access to government waste lands and legalised entitlements are restricted. Most of the land which was given to non-tribals under inalienable freehold title by proprietors of land tenures got legitimacy through subsequent state legal process of land claims during survey and settlement.

This study examines the cause of tribal land alienation in general; and the role of political and apolitical bodies, and Tribal Advisory Council in protecting the land rights of tribal peoples in the Scheduled Area. It also examines the historical evolution of the protective land laws as well as the forest laws, and outcome of legal proceedings against non-tribal occupants for restoration of lands, and the role of the judiciary in dispensation of justice. This study corroborates the reports on tribal land issues by the State level Tribal Welfare Department. This report explores how some of the major changes in the relationship of people with land have affected land administration systems and, further the role of land administration in tribal land alienation in the Scheduled Areas of the State.

Although Land Transfer Regulations 1 of 70 has been in force, its implementation is poor. The tribal land conflict resolution mechanisms have failed to restore the alienated lands to tribal people. The Regulations are inadequate to address the land rights of tribal people in the Scheduled Areas; administrative and legislative changes are required. The government is morally and politically obliged to rectify the legacy of tribals' dispossession of lands.

1

Tribal Identity and Land Alienation

1.1 Scheduled Tribes in Andhra Pradesh

Scheduled Tribes (STs) account for 8.6% of India's population. The term 'Scheduled Tribe', means any tribe or tribal community or part of, or group within any tribe or tribal community and specified as such, in relation to the State of Andhra Pradesh by Public Notification by the President under clause (1) of Article 342 of the Constitution. Thirty-five communities are notified in Andhra Pradesh as STs. Their population is 59.18 lakhs as per the 2011 Census. They constitute 7 per cent of the total population of the state.

The Tribal Sub-plan area extends over 31,485.34 sq. kms. in the districts of Srikakulam, Vizianagaram, Warangal, Visakhapatnam, East and West Godavari, Khammam, Adilabad and Mahaboobnagar districts constituting the traditional habitat of nearly 30 ST groups. The Yerukula, Yanadi and Sugali or Lambada live mainly in the plain areas outside the Scheduled Areas.

On the basis of geo-ethnic characteristics, the tribal areas of Andhra Pradesh have been divided into the following five geographical zones:

(i) The Gond region constitutes the tribal areas of Adilabad District in the extreme Gondwana region adjoining Maharashtra. The Gond community is sub-divided into six tribes: (i) Raj Gond or Gond, (ii) Pradhan, (iii) Toli, (iv) Dadve, (v) Gowari and (vi) Kolam. These communities are endogamous in nature.

(ii) The Koya-Konda Reddi region includes areas along the Godavari gorges, tribal areas of Karimnagar, Warangal, Khammam, West Godavari and East Godavari Districts. The Koyas are found along the Godavari River from Karimnagar to the East and West Godavari Districts. The Konda Reddis inhabit the banks on either side of the Godavari from Bhadrachalam area of Khammam district to Devipatnam and Polavaram areas of East and West Godavari respectively. Although they are spread over a large area, a majority of them are in Maredumilli and Addatigala region of the East Godavari District.

(iii) The Khond-Savara region constitutes those tribal areas which are part of the Eastern Ghats, spreading across the forest and hill tracts of Srikakulam to Vizianagaram and Visakhapatnam District. The origin of Savaras is traced to the ancient Sabars who are migrants from the lower reaches of the Ganges. The Savaras consist of two classes: Kapu Savaras who dwell in the plains, and Hill Savaras or Jati Savaras who consider themselves to be superior to their counterparts. The origin of the Khonds, however, is unclear. In the Visakhapatnam District Manual of 1869, they are recorded as owners and cultivators of the soil. They are divided into two groups namely, the Dongria Khonds and the Desys Khonds.

(iv) The Chenchu region comprises the tribal areas of Mahaboobnagar, Nalgonda, Kurnool, Prakasam and Guntur districts. The traditional habitat of the Chenchus is the contiguous forest tracts of Nallamalai Hills. Most Chenchus of this area are more or less at the food gathering stage of the economy. They largely subsist on hunting and collection of roots, timber and honey. However, although more than 18,000 Chenchus were enumerated in 1971, only a few hundred still pursue their traditional lifestyle as semi-nomadic forest dwellers.

(v) The Yanadis, Yerukulas and Lambadas inhabit the plains areas. These three groups have been recognised as STs in the Andhra region from 1956 and in Telangana from as late as 1976. The Yanadis are concentrated in the Andhra region, the Yerukulas throughout the state and the Lambadas, mainly in the Telangana region.

About two thirds of the STs of Andhra Pradesh live in the hilly and Scheduled Areas of Srikakulam, Vizianagaram, Visakhapatnam, East Godavari, West Godavari, Khammam, Warangal, and Adilabad Districts. After the Constitution of India came into force, these regions came to be known as the Scheduled Areas under a special order in 1953.[1]

Table 1: Location of Tribes in the Scheduled Areas of Andhra Pradesh

S.No.	*Name of the District*	*Scheduled Tribes*
1.	Srikakulam	Savara, Jatapu, Gadaba, Konda Dora.
2.	Vizianagaram	-do-
3.	Visakhapatnam	Bagata, Gadaba, Kammara, Konda Dora, Kotia, Khond, Mali, Manne Dora, Mukha Dora, Reddi Dora, Porja Valmiki, Gond, Kulia
4.	East Godavari	Koya, Konda Reddi, Kammara, Koya Dora, Valmikis, Konda Kapus.
5.	West Godavari	Koya, Konda Reddi, Yerukula, Yanadi
6.	Khammam	Koya, Konda Reddi
7.	Warangal	Koya, Lambada
8.	Adilabad	Gond, Kolam, Pradhan, Thoti, Lambada, Naikpod, Andh
9.	Mahaboobnagar	Lambada, Chenchu

Sources: Ashokvardhan, C. *Tribal Land Rights in India*, Centre for Rural Studies, LBS National Academy of Administration, Mussoorie, 2006.

1. Ashokvardhan, C. *Tribal Land Rights in India*, Centre for Rural Studies, Lal Bahadur Shastri National Academy of Administration, Mussoorie, 2006.

Fig. 1: Scheduled Areas of Andhra Pradesh

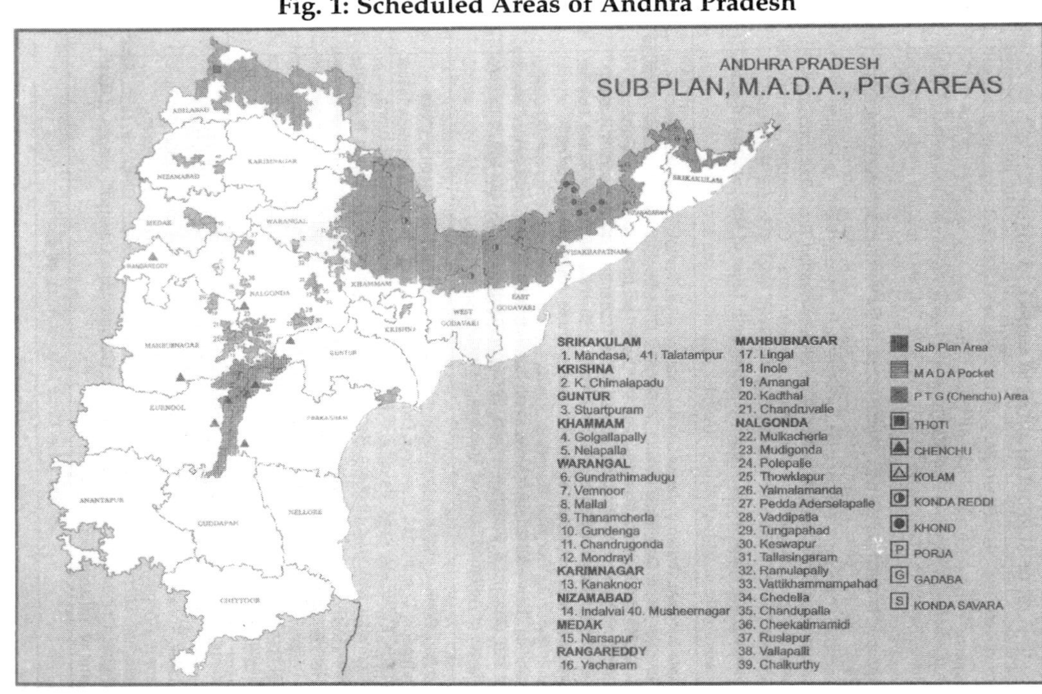

Source: *Basic Statistics on Scheduled Tribes of Andhra Pradesh*, TCRTI, Hyderabad, 2008.

1.2 Land Alienation Among Tribals

The question of land tenure has been a pivotal and sensitive political issue in the context of Scheduled Areas[2] of Andhra Pradesh. Agriculture continues to be the main source of livelihood for the majority of STs. However, large tracts of tribal land are in the hands of predominantly elite non-tribal sections of society. Consequently, STs are marginalised and deprived of their traditional land rights. The alien systems of land tenure introduced during colonial times have had far-reaching adverse effects depriving STs of their dignity and their access to land justice.

Historically, STs have had a rich cultural linkage with the natural resources. This relationship, however, was altered or even eroded with the arrival of the non-ST settlers from plain areas. The introduction of various land-related documents in tribal areas, and the imposition of unfamiliar modes of governance, began a cycle of land occupations by non-STs, legitimization of such legal occupations through land reforms, policy and law and finally, dispossession of STs from their control over land. Underlying these problems is a loss of identity and helplessness from having their values oppressed and their rights ignored. STs have restricted access to government waste land and legal entitlements. A large portion of the land which was given over to non-STs under inalienable freehold title by proprietors of land tenures got legitimacy through subsequent state legal process of land claims during the land survey and settlement operations.

From the tribal point of view, they suffer from several forms of alienation since, 'in a system of cumulative inequalities, privileges, property and power are combined in certain individuals, while the socially underprivileged are

---

2. Areas of Srikakulam, Vizianagaram, Visakhpatnam, East and West Godavari, Kammam, Warangal and Adilabad districts were notified by the President of India under the Fifth Schedule to the Constitution of India.

economically and politically deprived'.[3] Alienation of land itself, however, constitutes just a small component of this entire process of alienation, albeit an essential one. It is therefore imperative to view this single phenomenon within the holistic context of tribal existence and tribal cultural ethos.[4]

The alienation of STs from their traditional habitat is caused due to the policies of the State. The process of induction of non-ST population into these Scheduled Areas was expected to bring progressive assimilation of the local STs into the new socio-economic order of the immigrants, while raising their income, productivity and standard of living. 'However, often the outcome has been contrary to the above expectations, reducing the share of tribals in the gross regional product, substituting one institutional exploitation by another, uprooting them from their native land and reducing them to the status of aliens on their own soil.'[5]

In the early years of the 20th century, many ST communities lived by and large, freely in pre-capitalistic socio-economic formations[6]. This is because the community ownership of land in India was not commoditized prior to the British rule. STs in their pre-capitalistic socio-economic formations had not regarded land as a commodity as it was freely available to them for cultivation. Thus, the concept of

3. Beteille, Andre. *Studies in Agrarian Social Structure*, Oxford: Oxford University Press, 1974.
4. Philip Viegas. *Encroached and Enslaved*, Indian Social Institute, New Delhi, 1991, p. 32.
5. For details see, Patnaik, S.C. and S. Patel. Impact of Modernisation on Tribals: Economic Dualism and Path of Change (A case study of Malkangiri sub-division in Koraput district), paper presented at the Seminar on 'Prospectus of Economic Development of Tribals of Koraput District' held in October (Mimeo), 1982, pp. 2-14.
6. Satyanarayana, K. *A Study of History and Culture of the Andhras*, People's Publishing House, New Delhi, 1975, p. 44.

alienation with regard to the problem of land alienation in tribal areas can be understood in relation to the concept of private property relations, commoditization of the means of production as land, labour and capital and the very process of penetration of the private sphere by the state capital.

There were restrictions on STs on tapping toddy from any palm tree, and on the migration of castes who bought the licence to tap, distil and sell liquor. The distillers easily had the STs indebted to them, as the latter loved toddy, including taking of land in lieu of their petty debts. This was similar to the practice of the merchants and moneylenders, who had acquired ST land. Therefore the STs only lost more of their land to the non-STs in this process.[7]

Yet another form of land alienation is when the States promote development projects as hydroelectric power stations, mining and industries. These developmental activities do not confer any benefit on the STs directly and render them landless.[8] The construction of irrigation dams and industrialization are the major reasons for massive and irreversible deforestation and subsequent land loss of the ST communities. In the last sixty years, in the new era of development, ST communities have been displaced on a large scale. Displacement has taken place as an offshoot of the economic development by the State itself and, in particular, its industrialization and irrigation policy.[9] For instance, there are 18 major dams in Andhra Pradesh and six of the large ones alone have been responsible in displacing about half a million people. The proposed Indira Sagar Project (Polavaram) threatens involuntary displacement of 2.37 lakh

---

7. Rao, M.S.A. Non-tribal Colonisation and Tribal Deprivation in Andhra, *Social Action*, Vol. 33, July–September, Indian Social Institute, New Delhi, 1983.
8. *Draft National Policy on Tribals*, Ministry of Tribal Affairs, Government of India, New Delhi, 2004.
9. Rao, B. Janardhana. *Adivasis in India—Characterization of Transition and Development*, Adhyayana Publications, Warangal, 2000.

people from 276 villages in the Scheduled Areas of Andhra Pradesh, 55 per cent of them being STs. It will result in the submergence of 94,357 acres of land situated in the Scheduled Areas, of which 29,852 acres are *poramboke*. In addition to this, the Polavaram Project will submerge 3,223 hectares of forest.[10]

A review of literature on the subject provides a clear indication of the issues involved in landlessness and the magnitude of the tribal land alienation problem. The loss of private holdings by STs, despite a number of laws being passed by both the pre-colonial as well as post-colonial state to check land alienation, has been a cause of concern. These laws had many shortcomings and were unable to check the transfer of land from STs to non-STs.[11] Even where legislation is designed to protect tribal land interests, such as restricting alienation of ST land or ensuring that STs receive the benefit of land tenure reforms, the results have been disappointing.[12]

In many villages in the Scheduled Areas of the country, STs slowly lost their land to the non-ST moneylenders and landlords, reducing their status to that of tenants or labourers. In some places, the tribal chiefs were converted to Hinduism and they invited the non-ST peasants to settle in tribal areas. The latter being experienced farmers, seized the land from the STs and employed the natives as labourers.[13] Several legislations have been passed since independence, but 'despite the legislation in force against alienation of land from tribals to non-tribals, a fair proportion of them have either

---

10. Rao, Trinadha P. Nature of Opposition to Polavaram Project, *Economic and Political Weekly*, April 15, 2006.
11. Ambagudia, Jagannath. Tribal Rights, Dispossession and the State in Orissa, *Economic and Political Weekly*, August 14, 2010, Vol. xlv, No. 33, 2010.
12. Trivedi, H. *Tribal Land Systems: Land Reform Measures and Development of Tribals*, Concept Publishing Company, New Delhi, 1993.
13. Shah, G. *Social Movements in India: A Review of Literature*, Sage, New Delhi, 1990.

been dispossessed of their land or have parted with their land due to some other reason.'[14]

The tribal practice of shifting cultivation made the land that they relied on, vulnerable to settlement by immigrant farmers.[15] Unfortunately, despite most legislations being in place for more than forty years, restrictions on alienation have not been successful in protecting tribal land from alienation.[16]

A major consequence of loss of land is the growing number of agricultural labourers, an indication of the 'de-peasantisation' process.[17] In addition, the precarious economic circumstances of many STs have resulted in the chronic and continuing transmitting of tribal land to non-tribals.[18] Literature on tribal land alienation with regard to various governance structures and their impact on land alienation among ST communities under varied systems of land tenure are scanty. Several studies focused on the magnitude of land alienation in Agency Areas have drawn out the historical factors and political dimensions by documenting the struggles of tribal communities from pre-independence times to the promulgation of legislations and tribal development policies and administrative structures in the 1970s. Most of these studies provide insights into the magnitude of the tribal land alienation and de-peasantisation

---

14. Report of Commissioner for SC and ST (Fifth Report), Ministry of Tribal Affairs, GoI, Delhi, 1982-83, p. 28.
15. Bijoy, C.R. and K. Ravi Raman. Muthanga: The Real Story, *Economic and Political Weekly*, May 17, 2003, pp. 1975-80.
16. Reddy, Prabhakar T. Tribal Land Alienation in Andhra Pradesh, *Economic and Political Weekly*, Vol. 24, No. 28, 1989, p. 1573; and Karuppaiyan, E. Alienation of Tribal Land in Tamil Nadu, *Economic and Political Weekly*, September 9, 2000, p. 3350.
17. Manohar, K. Murali and Janardhan B. Rao. *Tribal Agricultural Labour: An Enquiry into the Depeasantisation Process in Tribal Transformation in India*, Buddhadev Chaudhari (ed.), Vol. I, Inter India Publications, New Delhi, 1992.
18. Baviskar, A. The Fate of the Forest: Conservation and Tribals Rights, *Economic and Political Weekly*, September 17, 1994.

process, the outcome of legal measures in restoration of the alienated tribal land, and the movement behind the promulgation of Land Transfer Regulations 1 of 70 in general. Available literature has perceived the tribal land alienation situation in a general manner giving greater attention to the magnitude of land alienation in the Scheduled Areas of Andhra Pradesh without examining the role of specific land tenure systems. The land administration practices have had diverse consequences on the process of land alienation in Agency Areas. Further, there is little awareness about the specific reasons for failure in restoration of the alienated tribal land and setbacks in the state policies and laws in addressing the tribal land rights issue. These studies are of limited help in explaining the actual causation and resultant factors with reference to different land tenure systems. How the varied land tenure systems affect the process of land alienation or restoration of tribal land is largely ignored as most of the studies have assumed that the structure of land relations are uniform across the state.

1.3 Tribal Identity and Land Rights

Tribal peoples share a symbiotic relationship with natural resources. Agronomic practices and their relationship with land are based on the nature-man-spirit complex and sustenance of the economy which is unique to tribal cultures in many parts of the country.[19] The interplay of nature and culture in their little traditions and the myriad ways in which

19. For instance, Vidyarthi, L.P. (1963) The Maler: The Nature-Man-Spirit Complex in a Hill Tribe introduces the concept of 'nature-man-spirit' in anthropology and Bharath Bhushan M. and Satyamohan, P.V. (1990) study of the tribal scenario in Andhra Pradesh, The Koyas—A Study of Nature-Man-Spirit-Complex among the Koyas of Bhadrachalam (mimeograph) explains the inseparable link of land with tribal life. The ethnographic film In Search of Ethnic Dimension—The Koyas made for the University Grants Commission deals with the nature-man interaction and the associated belief system. It

they have adapted to nature, indicates that tribal lifestyle, economy and social organisation 'are closely inter-related, interdependent and interacting' with nature and any interferences resulting in disturbances evokes severe resistance from the Adivasis. In the post-Independence decades, public and private enterprises encroached upon the Adivasi peoples' traditional domains, extracting minerals and timber and building dams and roads. Displaced in the name of progress, the Adivasis find their identities destroyed and their traditional livelihoods difficult to sustain.

Traditional communal land tenure systems continue to exist even where formal land tenure systems emphasise individual property rights.[20] In the predominantly agricultural societies, the importance of land cannot be over-emphasized. It is a symbol of security, the main source of income and wealth, as well as of social, political and economic power. 'The land tenure system reflects social class structure and class relations, as they represent an array of legal, contractual or customary arrangements whereby people engaged in cultivation, gain access to productive opportunities linked with land and thereby income.'[21]

Globalisation with its notions of private ownership reaches local communities largely through the market. In turn, the growth of the market has led to a process of privatisation of former communal land and devolution of ownership from community or clan to the family.[22]

---

examines the features of the environment in relation to the Koya economic system. Also see http://video.google.com/videoplay?docid=1204160986501454199&hl=en#

20. Roy Burman, B.K. *Communal Land System of the Tribals and Problems of Institutional Finance in Manipur and Tripura*, Delhi, 1986.
21. Morley, Mohan Lal. *Poverty Alleviation: The Indian Experience*. Himalaya Publishing House, Delhi, 1988, pp. 386.
22. Nathan, D.G. Kekar and P. Walter (eds.). Civilizational Change: Markets and Privatization Among Indigenous Peoples, in *Globalization and Indigenous Peoples in Asia: Changing the Local-Global Interface*, Sage Publications, New Delhi, 2004.

Tribal peoples suffer from physical displacement in several parts of the country owing to development projects initiated by the government.[23] Displacement among STs is on a massive scale and often with adverse implications on the communities, mainly due to laws that do not recognize the communal and customary rights of tribal people over their territories. Resettlement literature is replete with case studies on development projects that ignore the customary rights of the tribal people and treat them as illegal occupants of government land. Such an approach invariably leads to the impoverishment of once well-settled communities; precisely the opposite of what development promises.[24]

The Panchasheel of Pandit Jawaharlal Nehru laid the foundation of the State policy aiming to recognise the customary rights of Adivasis over natural resources. The tribal, who lives on a subsistence economy, perceives land primarily as a source of survival. On the contrary, for the non-tribal, it is the primary source of power and control and is understood as 'the ability to do things to others which you do not expect they can do on to you.'[25] It is acknowledged by

23. The Twenty-Ninth Report of the Commissioner of Scheduled Castes and Tribes (1990) says that even though tribal people form about 7.5% of the population, over 40% of the people displaced till 1990, belonged to these communities. A report of the Official Working Group on Development and Welfare of Scheduled Tribes during the Eighth Five Year Plan (1990-1995) on the rehabilitation of tribal people, based on a comprehensive study of 110 projects, has concluded that of the 1.694 million people displaced by these projects, almost 50% (814,000) were tribals.
24. Nath, N., D.K. Behera, and R.M. Sarkar (eds.). The So-called Development, Displacement and Dispossession: An Analysis on Land and Forest Rights of the Project Affected People, in *Land and Forest Rights of the Tribals Today*, Serial Publications, Delhi, 2006.
25. Desai, M., S.M. Rudolph and Ashok Rudra (eds.). *Agrarian Power and Agricultural Productivity in South Asia*, Oxford University Press, Delhi, 1984.

scholars that:

> Indigenous people often have a special relationship with the land—for many it is still their source of livelihood and sustenance and the basis of their existence as communities. The right to own, occupy and use land collectively is inherent in the self-conception of indigenous people, and this right is generally vested not in the individual but in the local community, the tribe or the indigenous nation.[26]

The British legal concept of individual private property destroyed the tradition of collective ownership and sharpened tensions within the Adivasi society while eroding their relationship with nature. These same tendencies are visible today in various developmental policies that are being implemented in the country in the post-independence era. It is the primary cause of conflicts between the STs and the larger non-ST society. The entire worldview of Adivasis is situated around their land. They cannot imagine their physical existence apart from it[27] and therefore eviction from their land or encroachments by outsiders has resulted in resistance and even armed struggles in Andhra Pradesh ever since the British era. There have been and continue to be, several rebellions across the country. Prominent among them in Andhra Pradesh are Alluri Seetarama Rao's armed resistance in Vishakapatnam Agency and the Gond Rebellion[28] led by Komram Bheem in Adilabad Agency in Nizam state. The Rampa Rebellion (1922-23) from East Godavari to Vizianagaram under Alluri Seetarama Raju were in protest of the Madras Forest Act of 1882 which placed restrictions on the free movement of STs in the forest areas

---

26. UNDP. *Human Development Report: Cultural Liberty in Today's Diverse World*, Oxford University Press, New York, 2004.
27. Pinto, Ambrose. Fillip to Land Transfers Land Acquisition Bill, *Economic and Political Weekly*, December 5, 1988.
28. Sastry, V.N.V.K. *Between Gonds Rebellion*, Udyama Publications, Hyderabad, 1989.

and prevented them from engaging in their traditional practice of *Podu* or slash and burn cultivation.

Post-independence, tribal unrest has been primarily on issues relating to restrictions on *podu* cultivation and encroachment of non-STs in large numbers into Agency areas, posing a threat to the existence and identity of tribal society. Bharath Bhushan observes that 'land alienation issues in agency areas have significant direct consequences to the demographic, political, ethnic, and gender aspects of tribal societies.'[29] Special laws to protect STs from land alienation have been violated and about 48 per cent of the land in Agency areas is formally owned by non-STs. Large scale manipulations during the Survey and Settlement period of 1970-76 led to grant of land entitlements of tribal land as settlement *pattas* in the name of non-STs. According to the Koneru Ranga Rao Land Committee Report, 'Every year more and more land is passing into the hands of non-tribals and if not checked with a very strong executive force, very soon the tribals may not have any land at all.'[30]

1.4 Fifth Schedule and Land Alienation

The future of land ownership and cultivation constitutes perhaps the most fundamental issue in national development. To a large extent the pattern of economic and social organisation will depend on the manner in which the land problem is resolved (First Five-Year Plan Document, 1951).

The Constitution of India enjoins upon the states, the obligation to promote the interests of Scheduled Castes and Schedule Tribes and to protect them from social injustice and all forms of exploitation. Land and land tenure are placed

29. Bhushan, Bharath M. *Land Rights of Women in Andhra Pradesh—A Status Paper* (mimeograph), Rural Development Institute, Hyderabad, 2011.
30. Ranga Rao, Koneru. *The Land Committee Report-2006*, GoAP, Hyderabad, 2006, p. 57.

under the exclusive legislative and administrative jurisdiction of the States. However, the Central Government has been taking on an advisory and coordinating role in the field of land reforms ever since the First Five Year Plan. However, for the land matters concerned with the Fifth Scheduled Areas, special provisions were made under the Constitution of India.

Article 244 is the most significant article in the Constitution regarding Adivasi rights. It states that the traditions and culture of ST communities are to be respected and the Scheduled Areas should function autonomously. The Fifth Schedule allows the President of India to declare areas as scheduled and gives the Governor of the State the power by public notification to not apply acts of Parliament or to modify them in accordance with the needs of STs. Crucially, the Fifth Schedule permits the Governor, on the recommendation of the Tribal Advisory Council, to prohibit the transfer of land by or amongst STs as well as to regulate the allotment of land to non-STs and the working of moneylenders.[31]

The Fifth and Sixth Schedules incorporated into the Constitution were specific to STs. The Fifth Schedule designates power to the President of India to declare certain areas as Scheduled Areas. The Scheduled Areas (Part 'A' States) Order, 1950 and the Scheduled Areas (Part 'B' States) Order, 1950 were issued declaring certain areas as Scheduled Areas in Part 'A' and Part 'B' States respectively. Part 'A' States refers to the Scheduled Areas of Andhra region while Part 'B' States refers to the Telangana region of Andhra Pradesh State. Through these orders, the provisions of the Fifth Schedule were made applicable to the Scheduled Areas of Andhra Pradesh. Article 244 of the Constitution of India states:

---

31. Bijoy, C.R. Adivasi Rights and Struggles of Autonomy: A Review of the Indian Experience in K. Krishnan (ed.), *Adivasi Groups* (Mimeo), 2000.

> Administration of Scheduled Areas and Tribals Areas. The provisions of the Fifth Schedule shall apply to the administration and control of the Scheduled Areas and Scheduled Tribes in any State other than (the States of Assam, Meghalaya, Tripura and Mizoram). The provisions of the Sixth Schedule shall apply to the administration of the tribal areas in the States of Assam, Meghalaya, Tripura and Mizoram.

Under Clause (5) of the Fifth Schedule, the Governor may by public notification, direct that any particular Act of Parliament or of the Legislature of the State shall not apply to Scheduled Areas or any part thereof in the State, or shall apply to the Scheduled Area or any part thereof in the State, subject to such exceptions and modifications as he may specify in the notification. The Governor may make regulations for the peace and good governance of any area in a State which is presently a Scheduled Area. In particular such regulations may,

(i) Prohibit or restrict the transfer of land by or among members of the STs in such area which is notified as Scheduled Area.
(ii) Regulate the allotment of land to members of the STs in such areas.
(iii) Regulate the carrying on of business as money-lenders who lend money to members of the STs in such areas.

All regulations made under this paragraph are to be assented to by the President for it to come into effect. If there is a Tribes Advisory Council for the State, no regulation shall be made under this paragraph unless the Governor making the regulation has consulted such a Council. Therefore, the Governor may make a regulation for the peace and good governance of a Scheduled Area in a state after consulting the Tribes Advisory Council of the State if one already exists.

In exercise of the powers conferred by paragraph 4(3) of the Fifth Schedule and in supersession of all the previous rules on the subject, the Governor of Andhra Pradesh outlined rules for the constitution of a Tribes Advisory Council (TAC) in Andhra Pradesh. These rules are known as the Andhra Pradesh Tribes Advisory Council Rules 1958. These rules came into effect from January 28, 1958. The TAC is to consist of 20 members of whom not less than 15 should be representatives of STs in the Andhra Pradesh Legislative Assembly. If the member representatives of the STs in the Legislative Assembly are less than 15, the remaining seats would be filled by other members of these tribes.

The members shall be appointed by the Governor by Notification in the Andhra Pradesh Gazette. The term of the Council shall ordinarily be three years. The Minister in-charge of the Welfare of Scheduled Tribes shall be the ex-officio Chairman of the Council. The TAC shall meet as often as are necessary and, in any case, not less than twice every year. The objective of the Council is to advise the Governor on matters pertaining to the welfare and advancement of STs.

Another important legislation which provides for the protection of tribal land, prevention of land alienation and restoration of alienated lands is the Panchayats (Extension to Scheduled Areas) Act, 1996 (PESA). This Act is in pursuance of the 73rd Amendment to the Constitution that makes it mandatory for all the States to enact panchayat laws for local governance. Recognizing that the Fifth Schedule Areas require a different frame of local governance, the 73rd Amendment exempts these areas from the application of the Amendment and required the Parliament to enact a separate legislation, the result of which is PESA. It provides for tribal self-rule on matters affecting tribal society and economy at the village level and enlarges the authority of local government to include various levels of control over local resources and programmes.[32] Andhra Pradesh enacted the Andhra Pradesh Panchayat Raj (Amendment) Act to incorporate PESA into its State law in 1998. However, this

---

32. Mahipal. Panchayats in Fifth Scheduled Areas, *Economic and Political Weekly*, May 6, 2006.

was not enabled through Rules for over a decade to even commence its operationalisation. The Rules were notified only in 2011. Its actual implementation is yet to be seen. "There are a number of inconsistencies between PESA and the state amendment. They also conflict with the State subject laws in a number of instances; for instance, PESA grants local communities the authority over resources which are in conflict with the existing state laws".[33] The PESA amendment to the State Panchayat Raj Act is not in total compliance with PESA.

The historical and legal perspective is that land in the Scheduled Areas once belonged to tribals. Until and unless the contrary is proved, the land in occupation by non-STs shall be deemed to have come through a transfer from STs. So the burden of proof lies on the non-STs to legally prove that the land in their possession had been with them even before the Andhra Pradesh Agency Tracts Land Transfer Act of 1917, which restricts land transfer between the STs and the non-STs. The STs have customary boundaries to the village and land is a community asset rather an individualized economic asset. The object of the Fifth Schedule and the Land Transfer Regulations is to preserve tribal autonomy and their culture, to help in their economic empowerment, to ensure social, economic and political justice for preservation of peace and good governance in the Scheduled Areas. The word 'regulate' in the allotment of land to members of STs in the Scheduled Area must be read as an endeavour to ensure regulation of the land only for and among the members of the STs in the Scheduled Area.[34]

---

33. Ramanathan, U. Common Land and Common Property Resources in Land Reforms in India, in *Issues of Equity in Rural Madhya Pradesh*, Praveen K. Jha (ed.), Vol. 7, Sage Publications, New Delhi, 2002, p. 204.
34. Samata vs. State of Andhra Pradesh, AIR 1997, p. 3301.

1.5 Non-tribals and the State in Scheduled Areas

Land of the tribal communities in this region has been taken away by the non-STs who have penetrated the region for economic gains. The penetration of non-STs was aimed at gaining access to forest and land to exploit them as economic resources, mainly for the market, thereby undermining the traditional subsistence economy and society of the tribal peoples.[35] This penetration was engineered by the British to serve their own colonial interest. Otherwise, there was no reason as to why a mass of non-ST people should suddenly begin encroaching upon tribal land, something they had not done in the past. The newly imposed British land system was radically different from that prevalent among many tribal groups.[36]

The colonial period witnessed a progressive and aggressive monetization of the economy of the tribal region for revenue generation, making dependence on the forest ever more precarious and thus destroying tribal self-reliance. Moreover, as the forests were taken over by government agencies and commercial interests, the tribal peoples were forced more and more to live by farming the land, where they were progressively pushed into bonded labour by exploitative landlords, moneylenders, government officials and other outsiders. The creation of private property rights over land was an equally disastrous break with Adivasi tradition in which land was always held by the community even when it was assigned for private use.[37]

The first phase of migration of non-ST peasants from the plains occurred around 1820 when a number of *zamindaris*, either whole or in part, came into the auction market and the

35. Arnold, David. Rebellious Hillmen: The Gudem Rampa Rising 1839-1924 in Ranajit Guha (ed.), *Subaltern Studies I*, OUP, Delhi, 1982.
36. Shah, G., op. cit.
37. Heredia, Rudolf C. Tribal History, Living Word or Dead Letter, *Economic and Political Weekly*, April 29, 2000.

highest bidder got the rights of ownership. This auction process was initiated to raise revenue. But it paved the way for the non-STs to infiltrate tribal areas. The administration further made steady inroads for the control of the productive resources of the STs by passing forest laws in 1882 and *abkari* laws in 1864. These laws were meant to regulate the forest usage and consumption of toddy or alcohol.[38]

However, the commercial penetration did not wait for the road building in the 1880s. Even before the Rampa Rebellion of 1879-80 in the Agency area of East Godavari district, traders and moneylenders were pushing into the hills and undermining the traditional economy. Malas, an untouchable caste, who in the lowland areas were among the most despised of Hindus, were quick to see the economic opportunities created by the more stable conditions of the 1850s and 1860s, and by the gradual extension of British control after 1848. Operating at first as petty traders and spending months on trading expeditions into the hills, they acquired the capital and expertise to develop into flourishing traders. They extended their activities to moneylending to cultivators and *muttadars*, and took over the hill villages as their own settlements. Komatis, the affluent and powerful trading caste in the plains who dominated commerce, especially the grain trade, followed the Malas. But unlike the Malas, they rarely lived in the hills, nor did they take trouble with petty trade. They sought the larger profits to be made from timber, opium and liquor or from the mortgaging of *muttadars'* estates in the Agency areas of Madras Presidency.[39]

The Godavari River facilitated the movement of non-STs from the widely populated plain areas of East and West Godavari to the sparsely populated tribal areas, by country

38. *Godavari District Gazetteer*, Government Press, Madras, 1907, p. 101.
39. Arnold, David, op. cit.

craft, mechanized boats and launches.[40] Towards the end of the 19th century, the British began leasing out the rights to extract bamboo and timber from the forests on both sides of the river to the non-ST merchants of Rajahmundry. When motor boats were introduced in the second decade of this century, a larger number of merchants and their agents moved into these settlements.[41]

With the attainment of independence, *zamindari* was abolished by the Estates Abolition Act XXV of 1948. In the 1950s, land in the Agency areas came into the open market. The non-STs owning land in vast stretches began to sell it in anticipation of the forthcoming land ceiling legislation. The stream of migration of the Kammas in the 1950s was different from the earlier migrations of other peasant castes before independence. While the latter was for subsistence, the former was for development. For instance, in Kanakapalli, a village located in the heart of the tribal area in the Buttayagudam block of Polavaram taluk, the Koyas own and cultivate only 17.4 per cent of the cultivable area of 2,910 acres, the rest being owned and cultivated by the non-STs. The Kamma migrants form the single largest group owning nearly 40 per cent of the total cultivable land. The village was first settled in 1899 for revenue when Koyas and the Koya Nayaks owned most of the land. In 1920, a rich zamindar from the delta area of West Godavari bought about 1,000 acres of semi-forest land of Kanakapalli to graze his large herd of cattle. Every year during July-November, a team of cowherds drove the herd over a distance of 40 miles when every inch of land in the delta area was covered with paddy.

40. Ashokvardhan, C. *Tribal Land Rights in India*, Centre for Rural Studies, LBS National Academy of Administration, Mussoorie, 2006.
41. Rao, Jayaprakash P. The Struggle for Land: Tribal Revolts in Two Villages, in K. Murali Manohar, P. Ramaiah and C. Sivaramakrishna Rao (eds.) *Political Economy of Tribal Development*, Indian Institute of Public Administration, Warangal, 1985.

The herd came back after the harvest when dry fodder became available.

Commercial crop tobacco replacing the traditional crops in the tribal areas witnessed a change. The tobacco rush resulted in both extension of commercialised agriculture by the farmers who had already migrated, and also a fresh wave of migration of non-ST farmers, either as transients (for the tobacco season) or as domiciles. However, for the STs, it meant further loss of land, control over life and exploitation by commercialised agriculture. Although the non-ST farmers were 'tenants' from the point of view of their tenurial position, they were the real exploiters in terms of production relations, reaping vast profits and the tribals, who were the land owners, became the exploited.[42] The penetration of the non-STs into the tribal areas with their capital and other instruments of exploitation including exchange of goods or giving money for exchange of goods not only destabilized the tribals' way of life but also affected their communal way of living.[43]

The huge influx facilitated further opening up of tribal areas intensifying the demand for land for diverse purposes— housing, infrastructure, business and social utilities which further led to the dispossession of the STs. For instance, if one travels by road through the long stretch from Bhadrachalam in the Khammam district of Andhra Pradesh to Raipur in Chhattisgarh, a distance of about 550 kms and almost entirely a Fifth Schedule region where ST land may not be sold or passed on to the non-ST people, yet, one can see that most of the shops and land along the roadside are

---

42. Rao, M.S.A. Non-tribal Colonisation and Tribal Deprivation in Andhra, *Social Action*,Vol. 33, July to September 1983.
43. Manohar, K. Murali. Political Economy of Tribal Development: A Theme Paper, in K. Murali Manohar, P. Ramaiah, and C. Sivaramakrishna Rao (eds.), *Political Economy of Tribal Development*, Indian Institute of Public Administration, Warangal, 1985.

owned or occupied by non-STs. This blatant encroachment upon tribal land is overlooked by a largely non-ST government that accepts tribal peoples' displacement as a precondition for development.[44]

The 1997 Samatha case in relation to permitting a private company for mining in the Scheduled Areas of Andhra Pradesh was a classic example of the State violating its own Constitutional duty in the Fifth Schedule Areas. In an effort to promote economic development through industrialization, the State has been allotting tribal land to private industries and developmental projects as mining, hydroelectric projects, industries and tourism.

With globalization, economic liberalization, attraction for direct foreign private investment and the availability of rich resources, the pace of takeover of tribal land has grown manifold, particularly by the industrial and mining sector.

1.6 Political Contestation Over Tribal Land Rights

In the absence of the operationalisation of PESA in the Scheduled Area, the political role of the Tribal Advisory Council (TAC) through their decisions in advising the government and Governor becomes a pointer to politics in the region. An analysis shows that several key decisions taken by the TAC were disregarded under political pressures from both ruling and non-ruling political parties in order to maintain their non-ST vote bank in the Fifth Schedule Areas of the State.

On the practice of some non-STs keeping tribal women as mistresses to grab their land, the TAC 'resolved to request the government (i) not to recognize the second marriage of a non-tribal with a tribal lady and to see that the land of tribals are not enjoyed by the non-tribals through such a marriage.'[45]

---

44. Ramnath, Madhu. Surviving the Forest Rights Act: Between Scylla and Charybdis, *Economic and Political Weekly*, March 1, 2008.
45. Minutes of Andhra Pradesh Tribes Advisory Council (37th) meeting held on February 5, 1977, Hyderabad.

However, this resolution has remained unimplemented. It was further resolved that the Andhra Pradesh Scheduled Areas Land Transfer Regulation, 1959 should be amended to declare the land purchased in the name of tribal women, married or kept as concubine by non-ST men, as null and void. There is a similar provision in the Orissa Scheduled Areas Transfer of Immovable Property (by Scheduled Tribes) Regulations, 1956.[46] But no amendment is made to the existing Land Transfer Regulations 1 of 70 laws to give effect to the recommendation of the TAC.

Yet another looming threat is the infiltration of relatively more dominant and powerful STs from plain areas into the Scheduled Areas and exploiting the land belonging to forest dwelling STs as there is no prohibition of land transfer amongst the STs. This has escalated inter-ST land conflicts. The TAC accepted the proposal to provide identity cards to the local STs as there are several cases of migration of non-locals into Andhra Pradesh, to corner the benefits extended to the local STs. This decision was made on the proposal of the Commissioner, Tribal Welfare, for banning alienation of land of Chenchus through an ordinance in view of their backwardness and presence of many young widows in Chenchu Project area as their spouses have probably died due to Tuberculosis or Cirrhosis.[47] In fact, no such mechanism is put in place to check the infiltration of non locals.

Even where land cases are successful, the aggrieved STs are unable to access the land owing to delay in execution of the orders issued in their favour by the Special Deputy Collector Court although instructions were given by the government to the authorities for the effective implementation of court orders through a circular No. 15857/ 79-C, 2 Revenue, Andhra Pradesh, Hyderabad, followed by

46. Minutes of the Andhra Pradesh Tribes Advisory Council Meeting Held on November 17, 1995, Hyderabad.
47. Minutes of the APTAC Meeting held on February 14, 1994 at 11 am at Telugu Samkshema Bhavanam, AP Hyderabad.

another circular Rc. No. JI/4206/79, dated October 17, 1979.[48]

The term 'transfer' under Land Transfer Regulations which prohibits ST land alienation, does not include testamentary disposition which means disposal of property through execution of a 'will'. This gives scope for further ST land alienation. In this backdrop, the TAC unanimously resolved to remove the term testamentary disposition of property by bringing in an amendment to the provision of Section 2 clause (g) with the word 'transfer' under Land Transfer Regulations.[49] However, this decision is not translated into action.

The TAC had also resolved to approve the amendment to the Regulations with retrospective effect stating that 'in view of the legal complication in implementing the Land Transfer Regulation in Scheduled Areas of Andhra Pradesh, it is desirable that the Andhra Pradesh Land Transfer Regulation 1959 which extended to Scheduled Areas of Telangana from December 1, 1963 may be amended so as to give retrospective effect from October 31, 1949', the date on which the Notified Tribal Areas Regulation came into force.'[50] But except for issuing a statement, no efforts were made to bring the legislation into effect from October 31, 1949 through an amendment to the law.

Regarding rehabilitation of *podu* cultivators, members of the TAC requested the concerned Ministry of Forests, Government of India, for early clearance of the de-reservation of an adequate extent of forest land for rehabilitating the Podu cultivation.[51] No such steps were taken to de-reserve the land. Instead, STs were evicted from the *podu* land in the Scheduled

48. Review of Action Taken on the Minutes of the Meetings of the APTAC (1979-80),Hyderabad.
49. Minutes of APTAC 102nd meeting held on March 18, 2010, Hyderabad.
50. Minutes of the 46th meeting of APTAC held on April 30, 1982, Hyderabad.
51. Minutes of the APTAC 52nd meeting held on November 28, 1986, Hyderabad.

Areas of Visakhapatnam district as per the Rehabilitation and Resettlement Action Plan (2002) of the Government of Andhra Pradesh.

As part of discussions on implementation of Land Transfer Regulations, all the members of the TAC unanimously approved the proposal in 1988 recommending amendment to all the regulations and other laws in the Scheduled Areas to restrict the power of stay of the Courts, including the High Court, and to specifically declare that no stay should be granted against the STs without hearing both the parties.[52] In fact, non-STs continue to obtain possession of land with the support of stay orders obtained from the High Court, stalling the implementation of the eviction order issued against them.

Government made an attempt to water down the Land Transfer Regulations of 1970 in 1988 by amending the regulation so as to permit the non-STs to transfer their land in the Scheduled Areas to other non-STs by sale. The then Chief Minister directed the Tribal Welfare Minister to steer the meeting of the TAC and get its endorsement for the amendment. Between December 1987 and March 1988, the TAC was convened four times for this purpose (usually it meets once in a year). To secure the ratification of the TAC, which is mandatory under the Fifth Schedule to proceed further in tribal affairs, the government brought strong pressure on the TAC in the form of a consensus resolution passed by the floor leaders of all political parties in a meeting convened by the Chief Minister on April 9, 1988.[53] Subsequently, the TAC was convened on May 10, 2000 to endorse the proposal to lease the land in the Scheduled Area for mining; but the TAC did not concede. The Chief Minister then summoned the Minister for Tribal Welfare and some

52. Minutes of the APTAC held on December 23, 1988, Hyderabad.
53. Reddy, Subba N. Depriving Tribals of Land—Andhra Move to Amend Land Transfer Laws, *Economic and Political Weekly*, Vol. XXIII, No. 29, 16 July 1988, pp. 1458-61.

other members of the TAC to persuade them on the benefits from leasing the land in the Scheduled Areas to a Dubai-based corporation for setting up an aluminium factory. Then a second meeting of the TAC was convened on May 24, 2000, where the majority of the members were finally bamboozled into toeing the government directive. However, the government decision was impeded by representations to the Governor and threats of legal action by human rights organisations, pro-ST non-government organisations and tribal groups.[54]

On the issue of Possession Certificates to non-STs, the TAC decided on July 12, 1999 on the resolution of May 9, 1998 approving construction of houses by non-STs in the Scheduled Areas.[55] This paved the way for issuing of a government order—G.O.Ms.No. 2 S.W. (LTR) Department dated July 1, 2000—approving the Andhra Pradesh State Housing Corporation Ltd. as a financial institution for the purpose of advancing loans to eligible non-STs in Scheduled Areas on mortgage of the super structure as security towards loans.[56] However, this decision was challenged by an ST, Tellam Venkata Rao and others before the High Court of Andhra Pradesh as it is against the provisions of LTR 1 of 70 in WP No. 3373/2000. The High Court struck down the contentious substance of the G.O. However the unsuccessful non-STs filed SLP No. 28423 of 2011 in the Supreme Court of India, which is pending for consideration.

A majority of the members, 10 of the 12 members of the TAC, supported the amendment to Land Transfer Regulation 1 of 70, enabling the State Government to acquire or grant any interest in the land including sub-soil rights for

54. Reddy, Subba N. Development through Dismemberment of the Weak—Threat of Polavaram Project, *Economic and Political Weekly*, April 15, 2006, p. 1430-1.
55. Minutes of the Andhra Pradesh Tribes Advisory Council Meeting Held on June 26, 1999, Hyderabad.
56. Minutes of the Andhra Pradesh Tribes Advisory Council Meeting Held on April 12, 2000, Hyderabad.

Reconnaissance Permit or Prospecting License or Mining Lease for major minerals, to any person or organisation, whether or not under the control of State or Central Government as suggested by the Advocate General of India.[57] However, the government could not bring the amendment due to strong opposition from tribal organisations.

While the TAC remains subservient to the State and the ruling class in general, even where positive decisions are taken, these are not implemented. TAC has not shown sufficient interest in the implementation of its own decisions.

1.7 Tribal Land Dispossession

Dispossession of land for a variety of reasons is evident, including for mines, industries, hydro power, and irrigation projects resulting in both direct and indirect eviction of the tribal communities.[58] The decline in the percentage of cultivators among the ST households from 45 per cent to 35.4 per cent during the period 1994-2005 indicates the loss of land and their increasing dependency on agricultural labour which increased from 37 per cent to 43.7 per cent during the period 1994-2005. The percentage of population depending on agricultural labour increased only in the case of STs, while it has declined for the Scheduled Castes.[59] Even the existing land holdings of the marginalised have been alienated despite a number of laws in force for ensuring protection of the land rights of the marginalised, especially the Adivasis.[60]

Had history been otherwise, nearly 5 lakh ST families living in the villages in the Scheduled Area of Andhra Pradesh would have presently together been the proud

57. Minutes of the meeting of the TAC held on May 24, 2000, Hyderabad.
58. Report of the Ministry of Rural Development, Department of Land Resources, Government of India, Delhi, 2000.
59. *Report on Human Development*, CESS, Begampet, Hyderabad, 2007.
60. Trinadha Rao, P. *Tribal Development in Question*, Laya Publications, Visakhapatnam, 2004.

owners of 18,48,209.30 acres of land with an average household landholding of 3.69 acres. But instead, more than 48 per cent of this land is cultivated by the non-STs. In some districts as Warangal, Khammam and Adilabad, more than 50 per cent of the land in the villages in the Scheduled Area is held by the non-STs. The pernicious poverty of the STs has led them to become victims of non-ST moneylenders resulting in indebtedness and consequent alienation of land. To check the land alienation, several Land Transfer Regulations including 1 of 59 as amended by 1 of 70, were created prohibiting the transfer of land between STs and non-STs, and among the non-STs since 1917. In spite of these restrictions, land alienation is still prevalent[61] amongst the Adivasis.

Table 2: Extent of Land under the Occupation of Non-Tribals in Scheduled Areas

S. No.	*Name of the District*	*Total Land in Scheduled Area in Acres*	*Land Under the Occupation of Non-STs in Acres*	*Percentage*
1.	Srikakulam	14949.17	359.20	2.20
2.	Vizianagaram	42333.00	91.00	0.21
3.	Visakhapatnam	288107.00	N.A	NA
4.	East Godavari	173417.49	33739.89	19.46
5.	West Godavari	75702.42	27979.16	36.96
6.	Khammam	771604.93	407368.33	52.79
7.	Warangal	142533.00	102104.50	71.64
8.	Adilabad	297170.95	180349.40	60.69
9.	Mahaboobnagar	42391.60	1444.18	3.41
	Total	1848209.56	753435.66	48.29 (excluding Visakhapatanam)

Source: *Report of Tribal Welfare Department*, Government of Andhra Pradesh, 1995.

61. Tribal Welfare Department, Government of Andhra Pradesh, Land Reforms and Land Transfers, *Report of Tribal Welfare Department*, Hyderabad, 1995.

The non-ST population which constitutes only 57.2 per cent in the Scheduled Areas of Andhra Pradesh demonstrates the inexorable influx of non-STs since the pre-independence era. The gravity of the tribal land alienation may be gauged from the fact that today non-STs own more than half of the land. The cultivable holdings of non-STs are 52 per cent in Khammam, 60 per cent in Adilabad and 71 per cent in Warangal Districts, despite the protective Land Transfer Regulations 1 of 70. These are official figures based on land records, and do not include other transactions as *benami* (fictitious) holdings.

Revenue records of 2007 show that in West Godavari District, STs have just 13,358 hectares of land while non-STs own 28,567 hectares of land. In Jelugumilli Mandal of West Godavari District, which has been a major conflict site, non-STs are reported to be controlling as much as 71 per cent of the land. In Khammam, non-STs are stated to own as much as 29,000 hectares of land.[62] What is significant is that STs have lost possession over the most productive land, and are left with poor quality land to cultivate.

A survey by the Human Rights Centre of Resource for Legal Action in 2002, on land leased out by STs to outsiders in the tribal *mandal* of Rampachodavaram in East Godavari District, provides information on unrecorded land alienation. This survey in 93 villages indicated that 355 STs gave away 1,797.50 acres on lease to the non-tribals to tide over the economic crisis in their families.

Land Transfer Regulations

In 1917, soon after a two-year long hit-and-run tribal insurgency in the Godavari Agency, the British enacted the first Agency Tract Interest and Land Transfer Act to prohibit land transfers between hill tribes and non-tribals without

62. Murthy, D.V.L.N. *Committee Report on Tribal Land Issues*, Ministry of Rural Development, Government of Andhra Pradesh, Hyderabad, 2005.

prior permission from the District Collector. Subsequently Land Transfer Regulations 1 of 59, as amended by 1 of 70, were made. Despite these being in force for long, 56 per cent of the cultivable land in the Scheduled Areas (about 8.7 lakh acres) is owned by the non-STs[63], while the extent of land restored to STs under these enactments is only 9 per cent of this area (about 80,000 acres). And, if anybody can ever manage to estimate the extent of agricultural land that is supposedly owned by STs but in reality is being held and cultivated by the non-STs, then these statistics would reveal an even more unequal state of affairs.[64] The Land Transfer Regulations 1 of 70 clearly states that the land in the Fifth Schedule Areas of Andhra Pradesh once belonged to the tribals. In this connection, it is important to see the extent of alienated land that was restored to STs and the effective enforcement of law.

The greater part of land alienation occurred after the 1940s. There are several loopholes in the existing Land Transfer Regulations 1 of 70. For instance, the law does not act retrospectively and thus cannot be applied to land transfer deals between STs and non-STs before the enforcement of the Act. Therefore, the exploitative relations in Agency areas still dominate the social structure. The problem of land alienation becomes part of the bigger problem of unequal class relations between STs and the non-STs in the present-day society.[65]

Further, the law protects only if the person belongs to a notified ST at the time when the transfer took place. The status of the person prior to the notification date would be non-ST. For instance, the Andhra Pradesh High Court held that on

63. Reddy, Subba N. Sword of Damocles Over Tribal People of Andhra Pradesh, *Economic and Political Weekly*, July 1, 1989, p. 1442-3.
64. Balagopal, K. Pitting the Tribals Against the Non-tribal Poor, *Economic and Political Weekly*, May 27, 1989, p. 1151.
65. Rao, B. Janardhana. *Land Alienation in Tribal Areas of Andhra Pradesh*, Kakatiya University, Warangal, 1987.

the date of transaction, October 20, 1917, the present Koya STs were not a 'hill tribe' within the meaning of the said expression in Section 2 of the Agency Tracts Interests and Land Transfer Act 1917. Thus the transfer between Koyas to non-hill tribes was not prohibited nor was it invalid when the actual transfer took place.

2

Land Alienation Under Different Tenurial Systems: Administrative and Legal Dimensions

2.1 Land Tenure Systems in Andhra Pradesh

'Land tenure systems' or 'land revenue systems' were brought in and systematically extended to cover the tribal habitations extending the scope of collection of land revenue. All cultivable land in British India fell under one of the three systems: landlord-based systems (also known as *zamindari* or *malguzari*), individual cultivator-based systems (*ryotwari*) and village-based systems (*mahalwari*).[66]

The land tenure systems varied over time in their form and institutions such as *muttadari, mokhasa, zamindari, ryotwari,* etc. They also differed from region to region. Besides being a source for revenue for administrative, military and other necessary expenditure, it also had anthropological, political and social dimensions. Land tenure rules set the platform for social and political institutions.[67]

---

66. Banerjee, Abhijit and Lakshmi Iyer. Colonial Land Tenure, Electoral Competition and Public Goods in India A Working Paper, January 2008 (see www.hbs.edu/research/pdf/08-062).
67. Ellickson, R. Property in Land, *Yale Law Journal*, 103(6), 1993, pp. 1344-62.

There are two important differences between the formal land tenure law and the customary land tenure law. The formal land tenure law involves the issue of land alienability or transferability of land. Most formal land tenure systems allow relatively unrestricted alienation of land rights, or at least do not normally distinguish between alienability within or outside a given social group. The customary land tenure law systems often prohibit the alienation of land rights to outsiders, but allow alienation within the group.

The second difference is the degree to which the land possessor may exclude others. The formal land tenure systems typically emphasize the right of right-holders to exclude others, whereas customary land tenure law more typically emphasizes inclusivity and the right not to be excluded.[68]

The concept of private property and a governance system to back it was introduced with the permanent settlement in 1793. This converted independent tribal landowners into tenants of *zamindars*. This exposed them to a multi-faceted exploitation which was beyond their capacity to handle[69]. Before the alien system of land ownership was introduced, commune or the common land holding, was the typical agrarian structure. The members of the community who were agnate, distributed the land among themselves according to individual needs and cultivated the allotted land on a co-operative basis. There was no system of measuring land for the sake of revenue collection. There was no authority to which any share crop was paid as tribute, tax or revenue. In course of time, this was replaced by individual land tenure under the overlordship of feudal chiefs. During this period,

68. Peters, P. The Erosion of Commons and the Emergence of Property: Problems for Social Analysis in Hunt, R.C and A. Gilman (eds.), *Property in Economic Context*, University Press of America, 1998, pp. 356-361.
69. Saxena, K.B. Development as Destitution: Disempowering Masses, *Alternative Economic Survey, India 2005–06*, 2006.

there were no intermediaries between the cultivator and the ruling chief because of the limited dimension of the kingdoms and direct contact of the chief with the peasantry.[70]

The British changed the Adivasis' relationship with the land, introducing the notions of individual property rights where there had been communal and occupancy rights, and production for profit where there had been a sustainable lifestyle. The British established links with local elites representing landholders, accountants, registrars and watchmen to consolidate their power. By doing so, they reinforced the semi-feudal agrarian system in place at the time and imposed a system of landlord and tenant where there was none. Towards the end of the 18th century, settlements were established to capitalize on the land and a revenue system that ignored the tribal tradition and customs.[71]

2.2 Land Tenure Systems in Tribal Areas

The proprietors of land tenures like *zamindari, muttadari, mahaldari and mukasadar,* were the principal intermediaries between the government and the cultivating peasants. *zamindari, muttadari and mahaldari* systems were abolished in 1969-1970, while the *mokhasa* system was abolished in 1989 in coastal Andhra. Thereafter its related Survey and Settlement Regulations were brought into force.

2.2.1 *Zamindari System*

The East India Company received the northern circars of southern Odisha (present Koraput, Ganjam and Phulbani districts) in 1766 as a gift from the successor of Salahar Jang, the Nizam Ali of Hyderabad. The Nizam asked the *Zamindar*

---

70. Mohapatro, Prafullo Chandro. *Land Revenue Administration in Tribal Areas in Economic Development of Tribal India,* Ashish Publishing House, New Delhi, 1987.
71. Jha, J.C. The Changing Land System of the Tribals of Chota Nagpur, 1771-1831 in Tarasankar Banerjee (ed.) *Changing Land Systems and Tribals in Eastern India in the Modern Period,* Subarnarekha, Calcutta, 1989.

Table 3: Typology of Land Tenures and Villages

Type of Land Tenure	*District*	*Taluks*	*No. of Inter-mediaries*	*No. of Villages*	*Areas in sq.kms*
Mahals	Kammam	Nugur	3	90	143.11
Muttas	East Godavari	Rampacho-davaram	24	174	297.97
		Yellavaram	11	228	294.35
	Visakhapatnam	Chintapalli	5	358	356.67
Estates	Vizianagaram	Parvathipuram	-	254	228.73
		Palakonda	-	4	9.07
	Visakhapatnam	Paderu	-	1373	888.58
		S.Kota	-	152	100.15
		Chodavaram	-	136	97.31
		Chintapalli	-	10	12.51
		Narsipatnam	-	3	3.15
	East Godavari	Devipatnam	-	19	101.63
		Yellavaram	-	2	2.62
	West Godavari	Polavaram & Buttayagudem	-	29	174.08
	Khammam	Bhadrachalam	-	358	795.00
		Nugur	-	112	202.00

Source: Notes-Agency Settlement Regulation, Tribal Welfare Department, Government of Andhra Pradesh, 1989.

of southern Odisha that they should regard the English Company as their sovereign in future, and to pay their rents and obedience to the said company or deputies without raising any trouble or disturbance.[72] However, there were a number of *zamindars* who opposed the Company Government and incited resistance. Much of the time and energy of the government had to be devoted to restore order.[73] After nearly four decades of British rule, the Madras

72. Matlhy, T.J. *Ganjam Manual*, Madras, 1918, p. 139.
73. Sardesai, G.S. *New History of the Marathas*, Bombay, Vol. II, 1948, p. 355.

Permanent Settlement Regulation was enacted in 1802.[74]

The revenue collection work by and through the landlords spared them the effort and expense of setting up a large administrative machinery. In these areas, the revenue liability for a village or a group of villages lay with a single landlord who was free to set the terms of revenue for the peasants under his jurisdiction and to dispossess any peasants who did not pay the landlord what they owed him.[75] The *ryots* (cultivators) were compelled to pay the government their entire paddy while themselves having to subsist on coarse grains. They also suffered constant ejectment from their holdings, and frequently resorted to borrowing from moneylenders to pay their *kistu* (payment of revenue on instalment basis) which fell due before the crop was ready.[76]

The drawbacks arising from these fluctuating and temporary arrangements came to an end with the introduction of the Permanent Settlement in 1802. The zamindars were now considered as proprietors of their estates upon a permanent *peshkash* per annum. Commenting on the merit of the settlement, Peter Cherry, the then Collector of Ganjam District in Odisha, remarked, 'I consider the introduction of permanent settlement as offering the only prospect of permanent peace and well-being to the tribals of Ganjam.'[77] However, the permanent settlement satisfied

---

74. Koraput district was part of Vizagapatam district of Madras Presidency and was not included in Odisha till April 1, 1936 when the province of Odisha was newly created. Ganjam district was also under the Madras Presidency till that date.
75. Kumar, Dharma (ed.). *The Cambridge Economic History of India*, Chapters I and II, Vol. 2, 1982.
76. Francis, W. *Madras District Gazetteers, Vizagapatnam*, Vol. I, printed by the Superintendent, Government Press, mimeographed copy, 1907, p. 310-11.
77. Yunus, S.A. *Orissa: Land Alienation and Restoration on Tribal Communities in India*, S.N. Dubey and Ratan Murdia (eds.), Himalaya Publishing House, Bombay, 1979, p. 140.

neither the *ryots* nor the *zamindars,* and chronic disturbances broke out in Koraput as well as in Ganjam district.[78]

In 1832, the disturbances in the district and in the Parlakhemundi *zamindari* of Ganjam rose to such a height that the government was compelled to appoint Russell as Special Commissioner, arming him with extraordinary powers and a large military force to suppress the revolt.[79] In 1939, on his advice, the Act XXVI was passed. According to this Act, 7/8th of the district was removed from the operation of much of the ordinary laws and administered directly by the Collector with special powers. Thus, the British Government deferred the operation of the permanent settlement among the hill-chiefs.

2.2.2 Ryotwari System

The first major shift away from landlord-based systems was in the Madras Presidency, where the administrators, Captain Alexander Read and Sir Thomas Munro, began advocating the establishment of an individual cultivator system in the late 1890s. Under this *ryotwari* system, the revenue settlement would be made directly with the individual *ryots* or cultivator.

With the failure of the Permanent Settlement Act of 1802-1803, the old *zamindaris* were parcelled into small blocks and sold for arrears. In the absence of bidders, the government took possession of them, and made a survey of land and settled them. Thus, the first *ryotwari* settlement was carried out in 1809 and a resettlement was done in 1933. The government villages were called *izara* villages and revenue was collected directly through the village *munsif,* who was assisted by the village accountant known as *karnam* and servants known as *talaris*. Thus, in the Polavaram taluk, different kinds of tenure villages coexisted: there were the

78. Senapati, N. and N.K. Sahu. *Orissa District Gazetteers,* Koraput, O.G.P., 1966, pp. 70-1.
79. Francis, W., op. cit., pp. 318-9.

zamindari villages, *inam* villages and land, *agraharam* villages (villages granted to Brahmins) and *izara* villages. The cultivators, merchants and others who had influence with the administration could move into the Agency area and 'buy' land with permission from the administration. Rich *zamindars* from the delta area bought large chunks of land in the semi-forest area in order to graze their cattle. Thus, the *izara* and *zamindari* villages received more migrants consisting of peasants and labourers from the plains.[80]

2.2.3 *Muttadari System*

Mutta means a village or group of villages held by a *muttadar*. *Muttadar* means a person who holds a *mutta* under a *sanad* granted by the government, subject to the payment of a fixed amount of land revenue to the government. The muttadar assisted the government in maintaining law and order in the *mutta* and includes his succession in interest. This means the rights and control over the *mutta* devolves through succession to his successors.

The *muttadari* system provided an institutional structure that formally united the various hill communities. Its origins cannot be stated with any certainty. According to Haimendorf, it was introduced into Rampa by the Reddi kings of Rajahmundry during the 14th century. As the term is Persian and Urdu, it might have been applied to an already established arrangement during the period of Muslim rule from Golconda (1571-1686).[81]

The *muttadari* land tenure system continued during the British times. In deciding to restore Rampa to the *mansabdari* family, the Board of Revenue of the Madras Government

80. Rao, M.S.A., op. cit.
81. Haimendorf, Furer. *Tribes of India: The Struggle for Survival*, Oxford University Press, New Delhi, 1985. pp. 203-8; F.R Hemingway, *Madras District Gazetteers: Godavari*, 1915, p. 67; Thurston, *Castes and Tribes*, III, p. 355. IV, pp. 64-5; Cain, *Bhadrachellam and Rekapalli Taluqas*, p. 33.

observed in 1848, that 'tracts such as that under consideration —wild and unproductive—and which, from the character of the country and climate, must be difficult of management by the officers of government, are always best confined to the administration of their native chiefs.'[82] Thus, the difficulties of external control over the hills forced the Madras government to follow the earlier expedient of indirect control through the *Muttadari* system.

The *muttadari* system was needed by the pre-colonial and colonial states at a time when land revenue and related taxes were a major source of income for the ruling classes. The STs hated it, both for the plunder it entailed and the oppressive practices the *muttadars* developed using their power.[83]

A study in Adilabad, Cuddapah and East Godavari districts of Andhra Pradesh, where 430, 370 and 248 persons belonging to STs were interviewed, revealed that indebtedness of STs was mainly responsible for the existence of the *muttadari* system.[84] Recommending the abolition of the *muttadari* system in 1951, the team of experts headed by R.S. Malayappan, Special Agency Development Officer, said that the 'The *muttadars*, at least, some of them are still enforcing '*vetti*' or forced labour and appropriating to themselves the best lands in every village of *mutta*. So long as they exist, they will not allow the hillmen to come up.'[85]

This system is one of the main causes of land alienation. Under the *muttadari* system, the tribes used to pay *mamool* or

82. Arnold, David. Committee of Circuit's Report, 1787, cited in Ranjit Guha, Rebellious Hillmen in *Subaltern Studies-I*, OUP, Delhi, 1986, p. 4.
83. Balagopal, K. (1989), op. cit.
84. Murthy, Linga N. and C. Shiva Rama Krishna Rao. Debt-Bondage in Tribal Areas—An Empirical Observation in K. Murali Manohar, P. Ramaiah and C. Sivarama Krishna Rao (eds.) *Political Economy of Tribal Development*, Indian Institute of Public Administration, Warangal, 1985.
85. *Report of the Study Team on Social Welfare and Welfare of Backward Classes*, Vol. I, 1959.

rent to the muttah-heads who in turn paid *kattubadi* (payments made as land revenue for the land held) to the muttadars, who then paid a fixed annual tribute known as *peshkash* to the British Government. The rate and type of *mamools* were arbitrarily fixed. They were not proportionate to the legitimate rise in proceeds and extension of cultivation. The attitude of the tribals towards the excessive demand by the *muttah*-head was one of complacence and mute submission.

Under this land system, the muttadars and *mutta*-heads had no power to eject the ryots and enhance '*mamools*' or rents, for neither had the rights of transferring a piece of land in the Agency Areas from the STs to the non-STs. But these principles were frequently violated in practice. The non-STs, who were employed in the offices of *muttadars* and *mutta*-heads, were given land grants for the services they rendered, and all the land belonged to the STs. During the period, the area was sparsely populated and land was available in plenty. The dispossession of STs from their land did not pose any serious problems to them. A dispossessed tribal could readily shift to a new area, bringing it under cultivation and cultivated it until he was again evicted by a *muttadar* or *mutta*-head.[86]

2.2.4 Mokhasa System

The definition given to *mutta* was extended to the *mokhasa* system. This system was abolished in 1989 and the provisions of the *muttadari* system for survey and settlements were extended to the Fifth Schedule Areas.

2.2.5 Mahals System

In the *mahal* land tenure system, the *mahaldar* is head of the *mahal* which is a constituent of a few notified estates. However, the *mahal* system was abolished by the Government of Andhra Pradesh and the Mahals Regulations

86. Balagopal, K. (1989), op. cit.

1 of 1969 was introduced for determination of land rights of cultivators. For the purpose of these Regulations, *mahal* refers to the Nugur, Albaka and Cherla estates and includes the area comprised in each of the villages of Subbannapeta, Dandupeta and Sarangapani, but did not include a survey number as per the definition given under Section 2(d) of the Andhra Pradesh Mahals (Abolition and Conversion into *Ryotwari*) Regulation 1/1969.

Regulation 1/1969 was enacted to abolish the *mahaldari* system prevailing in the Agency areas of erstwhile Nugur Taluk in Khammam district, and came into force on December 26, 1970. The Director of Survey, Settlements & Land Records was appointed under Sec. 4(1) to carry out survey and settlement operations and to introduce the *ryotwari* settlement in the *mahal* villages.

2.3 Land Reforms

The earliest initiative in land reforms was in the form of the Madras Estates Land Act of 1908 enacted to ensure that as long as the tenant paid the share of cultivation, he could not be evicted from tenancy. This provision was made uniformly applicable to all areas and failed to make any special considerations for STs. The non-STs who migrated to tribal areas took advantage of this provision during the land surveys carried out in 1902 and 1932-35, and got their lands surveyed in their favour as there is no specific bar on non-STs' acquisition of lands in tribal areas. In the 1934 survey, 351 non-STs were given land entitlements (*pattas*) for over 98,000 acres in East Godavari District Agency Area. By this time there were no stringent laws that protected the interest of STs from exploitation by the non-ST groups. STs claim that more manipulations took place during the survey conducted in 1934 rather than in 1919. Names of non-STs as cultivators were incorporated in land records. Subsequently, non-STs claimed land rights on the basis of such fraudulent entries in the revenue records. These entries became hurdles in the implementation of tribal protective land laws.

The earliest reform introduced in the Nizam's Dominions

was the Prevention of Alienation of Agricultural Land Act of 1349 F (1939-40). The Act applied to the non–Diwani territories also and empowered the government to notify from time to time, what was described as the agricultural class. Members of this class were required to obtain the permission of the *taluqadars* to alienate agricultural land permanently. Tenants who were in continuous possession of land for a period of six years during 1932-1942 and who had personally cultivated those stretches of land during this period were afforded protection by the Agricultural Tenancy Act. These Acts were, however, not implemented effectively and hence the benefits under the Acts did not in fact materialize so far as the tenants were concerned. The dichotomy between ownership and cultivation of the land became increasingly pronounced.

The abolition of *jagirs* in 1949 under the Hyderabad (Abolition of Jagirs) Regulation was a major reform undertaken by the Government of Hyderabad. The Hyderabad Tenancy and Agricultural Land Act 1950, based on the recommendations of the Agrarian Reforms Committee of 1949, provided for improvement of the status of tenant, limitation of the size of holdings, abolition of absentee landlordism, reduction of rents and imposition of restrictions on resumption of land for personal cultivation. The records of ordinary and protected tenancy rights were prepared and certificates were issued to approved tenants.

The other measures taken by the Hyderabad Government were the passing of an amendment to the Land Revenue Act of 1317 F(1907-08) in 1952 to provide right of ownership to *Shikmidars* in Ijara Izra and Banjara villages and the stoppage of cash grants like *rusums* and *mansabs* for institutions like the Deshmukhs and Deshpandes. The Hyderabad Abolition of the Inams Act of 1955 provided for the abolition of *inams* and conversion of their tenure into *ryotwari*. This Act was however not enforced properly and hence the Andhra Pradesh (Telangana Area) Abolition of Inams Act of 1967 was passed.[87]

87. *AP District Gazetteers*, Government of AP Press, Hyderabad, 1976.

2.3.1 Abolition of Intermediaries and Operational Issues During Land Surveys

The land surveys carried out at various points of time ended with a provision for land rights to non-STs in the Scheduled Areas. The land reforms, more particularly the abolition of intermediaries and settlement of land rights in favour of *ryots*, turned out to be beneficial to the non-STs.

Verrier Elwin, the anthropologist, who had warned about the possible dangers of the lack of proper maintenance of land records, had observed that 'in most of the inaccessible and ex-*zamindari* areas, no proper records of rights had been prepared.'[88] The unclear state of land records, both in the initial stages of the survey and the settlement operations undertaken in the British period during 1932-35, and in the period following the plain area regular settlement operations, exacerbated the issue of land alienation in tribal areas. The National Commission on Backward Areas (1981) observes that 'a significant consequence of the unsatisfactory state of land records was that the tribals were never legally recognised as owners of the land which they had cultivated, since they could only continue to occupy the area till a superior claim to the land was initiated.'[89]

Table 4: Laws Applicable to Agency Areas

Sr.No.	*Short Title or Subject*	*Year*
1	The Ganjam Vizagpatnam Act	1839
2	The Scheduled Districts Act	1874
3	The Nugur Albaka and Cherla Laws and Cesses Regulations	1909
4	The Agency Tract Interest and Land Transfer Act	1917
5	The Andhra Pradesh Agency Rules	1924
6	The Government of India Act	1935

88. Elwin, Verrier. *New Deal for Tribal India*, Ministry of Home Affairs, New Delhi, 1963, p. 49.
89. *National Commission Report* on *Backward Areas Development*, June 1981, p. 50.

7	The Tribal Areas Regulations 1359 F	1949
8	The Constitution of India	1950
9	The Andhra Pradesh Scheduled Areas Land Transfer Regulations 1 of 59	1959
10	The Andhra Pradesh Scheduled Areas Debt Relief Regulations	1960
11	The Andhra Pradesh Mahals (Abolition and Conversion into Ryotwari) Regulation 1 of 69	1969
12	The Andhra Pradesh Muttas (Abolition and Conversion into Ryotwari) Regulation 2 of 69	1969
13	The Andhra Pradesh Scheduled Area Land Transfer Rules	1969
13	The Andhra Pradesh Scheduled Areas Money Lenders Regulations	1970
14	The Andhra Pradesh Scheduled Areas Land Transfer Regulations 1 of 70	1970
15	The Andhra Pradesh Scheduled Areas Ryotwari Settlement Regulations 2 of 70	1970
16	The Andhra Pradesh Scheduled Areas Land Transfer Regulations 1 of 71	1971
17	The Andhra Pradesh Scheduled Areas Land Transfer Regulations 1 of 78	1978
18	Andhra Pradesh Panchayat Raj (Amendment) Act	1998

2.4 Survey and Settlement Regulations

After abolition of intermediary land tenure systems, survey and settlement operations work was undertaken in the Agency Areas of Srikakulam, Vizianagaram, Visakhapatnam, East Godavari, West Godavari, Nugur and Bhadrachalam taluks of Khammam district of the Andhra region.

The survey and settlement operations are covered by Andhra Pradesh Regulations 1/69, 2/69 and 2/70, to settle the land occupations of both STs and non-STs. Three tenures, viz. *malguzari, muttadari* and estates, prevailing in these areas were converted into *ryotwari*. The intermediaries, *mahaldar, muttadar* and *zamindar* between the government and *ryots* were abolished. The three regulations are:

- Andhra Pradesh Mahals (Abolition and Conversion into Ryotwari) Regulation 1969 (Andhra Pradesh Regulation

1/69): This Regulation abolished *mahals* in the Scheduled Areas of Nugur, Albaka and Cherla in Khammam district and their conversion into *ryotwari* land. It came into force on December 26, 1970.

- Andhra Pradesh Muttas (Abolition and Conversion into Ryotwari) Regulation 1969 (AP Regulation 2/69): This Regulation abolished *muttas* in certain Scheduled Areas as Paderu in Visakhapatnam district and Rampachodavaram in East Godavari district. It came into force on December 26, 1970. The purpose of the notification was to vest all rights and interests of *muttadar* in the government, free from all encumbrances. The regulation provided that the government shall not dispossess any person of any agricultural land if he is prima-facie entitled to a *ryotwari patta* pending a final decision. The non-ST ryot has to also prove that his possession and occupation over the land claimed was not void or illegal under the Andhra Pradesh Scheduled Areas Land Transfer Regulation 1959 (Regulation 1/59) or any other law. The ST ryots in occupation of *ryotwari* holdings for a continuous period of not less than one year would be entitled to a *ryotwari patta*, whereas a non-ST ryot is not entitled to a *patta* unless he is in lawful possession for a continuous period of 8 years immediately before the notified date and such possession and occupation was not attracted by Land Transfer Regulations 1 of 70. No *ryotwari patta* would be granted for land that exceeds 10 per cent gradient in respect of communal land. These regulations restrict the ryots from seeking *patta* over the forest land. The Government of Andhra Pradesh appointed Settlement Officers to conduct survey and settlement operations in the Pamuleru *mutta* between 1970-76 and granted settlement *pattas* to STs who had been in possession and enjoyment of land prior to the notified date of the regulations.
- Andhra Pradesh Scheduled Areas Ryotwari Settlement Regulation 1970 (Andhra Pradesh Regulation 2/70):

> This Regulation provides for the ryotwari settlement of certain lands in the Scheduled Areas in the Andhra area in respect of which no settlement has been effected, i.e. part of Khammam, Srikakulam, Vizianagaram, Visakhapatnam, East Godavari and West Godavari districts. It came into force with effect from July 1, 1971.

All the Estates in the Scheduled Areas were brought under these Regulations. These Regulations do not permit grant of *patta* in land exceeding 10 per cent gradient. The Settlement Officer has to conduct an enquiry into the nature of all lands to which *patta* is claimed to decide claim for which land shall be allowed and the person entitled to *ryotwari* settlement *patta*. These Regulations, while attempting to end the feudal system of administration of land, also opened the floodgates for non-STs to claim legal rights over tribal land in Scheduled Areas.

All the Settlement Regulations referred to above, in fact, dilute the letter and spirit of Land Transfer Regulations 1 of 70 by enabling non-STs to claim *patta* over land situated in the Scheduled Areas, in effect negating the presumption that unless and until the contrary is proved, the land in occupation by non-STs would be deemed to have come from STs through a transfer.

The Expert Group on Prevention of Alienation of Tribal Land and its Restoration, Ministry of Rural Development, Government of India, headed by the Planning Commission Member, B.N. Yugandhar, has also cast serious doubt on the settlement *patta* throughout the Schedule Five areas. Similarly, the denial of *pattas* to STs is the other side of the coin of Settlement *pattas*, which calls for a scrutiny of the rejection orders.[90]

According to the 1990 Report of Neerabh K. Prasad, an IAS Officer, titled 'Protection of Tribal Land' in the Settlement Regulations 2/69 and 2/70, it eas stipulated that the non-

90. *J.M. Girglani Commission Report*, Ministry of Rural Development, Government of Andhra Pradesh, 2005.

STs had to prove eight years of continuous possession of land prior to 1969 and 1970 and an absence of any prohibited transfer as per Land Transfer Regulations, to be eligible for a grant of a *patta*. Further, it states that norms were openly flouted by the non-STs. False receipts were created by the *mutta* clerks or estates clerks showing payment of taxes. The STs were driven out by creating terror through organising police raids, thus making it convenient for the non-STs to get the ST land measured in their names. In a specific case at Nelakota village of East Godavari District, the village abuts a huge inland tank by the name of Ramavarapu Ava and gets irrigation from the same. The non-ST residents of the adjacent villages, especially Ramachandrapuram, dubbed the STs as Naxalites (post-1969 Srikakulam Naxalite Movement period) and organised police raids. The STs had to flee from the hill tops and stayed there for more than a month. This period was used by the non-STs to get the land surveyed and settled in their favour. Land with rich forest growth was taken as *patta* even though STs were never in occupation of the land; obviously with an eye to the rich timber. The cases of Jangalthota and Chintalpudi of Y. Ramavaram Mandals of East Godavari are glaring examples of these. The tribal claims were never properly examined and were largely unaware of the settlement operations. By the time the STs realized that their land was being granted as *pattas* to the non-STs, it was too late for an appeal. As a result of these dubious measures, the land holdings of the non-STs jumped from 9,805 hectares before 1969 to 16,789 hectares by 1976 in the Scheduled Area of East Godavari District.[91] The non-STs in three Agency mandals of West Godavari District hold *pattas* for over 53,719 acres, while the STs have *pattas* for over 37,042 acres only in the Scheduled Area as per the Minutes of the Cabinet Sub-Committee circulated on July 24, 1997:

91. Rao, Trinadha P. Persisting Alienation of Tribal Land, *AP Social Watch Report*, Hyderabad, 2007.

> Just before the abolition of the Estates, the land holders accelerated issuance of *pattas* in several cases even with regard to the waste land in the estates by receiving paltry sums. So the Settlement Officer is directed to reopen all the *pattas* that were granted till now under the provisions of Ryotwari Settlement Regulations 2 of 1970, observed by Justice B.S.A. Swamy while dealing with a case in relation to land disputes in West Godavari District Agency Areas.[92]

In Bhadrachalam division in Khammam district, 8,297 non-STs were granted *pattas* for 29,554.16 hectares according to the Report of Secretary to Government (1992). Expressing concern over the grant of *ryotwari* settlement *pattas* to non-STs in the Scheduled Areas during the survey period, the Secretary to Government, Govindarajan (1992) reports:

> Two cases have come to the attention of the Government during the course of verification by special officer for survey of tribal land and assignment to tribals in Khammam district in the month of July 1990. In one case five non-tribals were granted *ryotwari patta* in respect of an extent of 30 acres of land while the tribals are in possession and enjoyment of the said land. In another case, non-tribals have obtained *ryotwari pattas* in respect of an extent of 101 acres where as the tribals are in continuous occupation and enjoyment of the said land.

There is another important legislation in respect of lands in the Telangana area of the State. The Andhra Pradesh (Telangana Area) Tenancy and Agricultural Land Act of 1950 classifies all tenants into ordinary and protected tenants. The Act further stipulates that if the tenant personally cultivated the land continuously for a period of six years during a stipulated period, he shall be deemed to be a protected tenant. As a protected tenant he reserves the right to purchase the land from the owner. This Act was also in force in the tribal areas of Telangana region. The non-STs who gained access to land from STs through clandestine and dubious methods were protected by the legislation. There was no law strictly

92. P. Gangamma vs. Vasudha Misra & Another. 1998(2) ALD 35.

prohibiting the transfer of land between STs and non-STs till 1963 in the Telangana region barring a revenue division Bhadrachalam in the Kammam district. The land reforms which were introduced by the State of Andhra Pradesh protecting the tenancy was made applicable to tribal areas without taking into cognizance the tribal interest.

During 1996-1997 when land disputes erupted in tribal areas of West Godavari District, one of the major contentions of STs was that they should be given possession of land as per the 1902 Resettlement Register (RSR) and the non-STs who were occupying land classified as tribal or government in the 1902 Resettlement Register should prove that they got hold of the land in a legal manner. The Resettlement Register of 1902 is currently not even available with the offices of the Commissioner, Tribal Welfare or the district.[93]

Land reforms focus on individual *patta* while much of the tribal land is communally owned. It can, therefore, be declared State property according to the present law and taken away from STs. Such alienation is clearly visible in the forest management system and development-induced displacement. Other processes of land transfers with the intervention of non-STs supplement it.[94]

The State, by introducing the land record system, helped legalize the then existing land relations ignoring the claims and prospects of the real 'owners'. Thus, not only did land become alienated, but the state itself became 'alien' to STs with its anti-ST activities.[95]

---

93. Note on Land Problems in Agency Areas of West Godavari, Social Welfare (TW) Department, Government of AP, Hyderabad, 1997.
94. Fernandes, Walter. Land Reforms, Ownership Pattern and Alienation of Tribal Livelihood, *Social Action*, Vol. 46, October-December 1996, pp. 428.
95. Rao, B. Janardhana (1987), op. cit.

2.5 Historical Evolution of Land and Forest Laws in Fifth Schedule Areas

A brief historical overview of the legislations affecting the ownership and management of land and forest in Scheduled Areas is essential to appreciate the pattern of the growing problem or the continued struggle for tribal land rights. Such a critical assessment in Agency areas with a historical perspective in two phases, viz. pre-independence and post-independence era, demarcates the major concerns and issues.

2.5.1 Pre-Independence Period

George Russell, a member of the Board of Revenue, in the then Government of Madras was appointed in 1822 to study the socio-economic situation in the tribal areas of Ganjam and Vizagpatnam districts. The Ganjam and Vizagpatnam Act 1839,[96] was the result of the realization that tribal areas had to be administered separately. The responsibility for the administration of both civil and criminal justice was entrusted with the District Collectors as Agents to the state government. The areas that they governed were called 'Agency Areas'. However, the measures taken by the government in relation to the administration of the justice did not improve the situation in the tribal tracts. Several rebellions ensued. In the wake of widespread unrest in the tribal areas of northern most districts of the then Madras Presidency, the government enacted the Ganjam and Vizagpatnam Act 1839, under which the tribal areas were removed from the purview of general laws. The enactment was made to provide for the administration of justice and for collection of revenue in the Agency Areas. As certain doubts had arisen as to which Acts or Regulations were in force in some parts of British India, the Scheduled Districts Act XVI of 1874 came to be passed. Tribal areas were constituted into 'Scheduled Districts'.

The British first recognised land alienation as a pressing

---

96. Presently Srikakulam, Vijayanagaram and Visakhapatnam Districts.

Fig. 2: Agency Areas of Andhra Pradesh

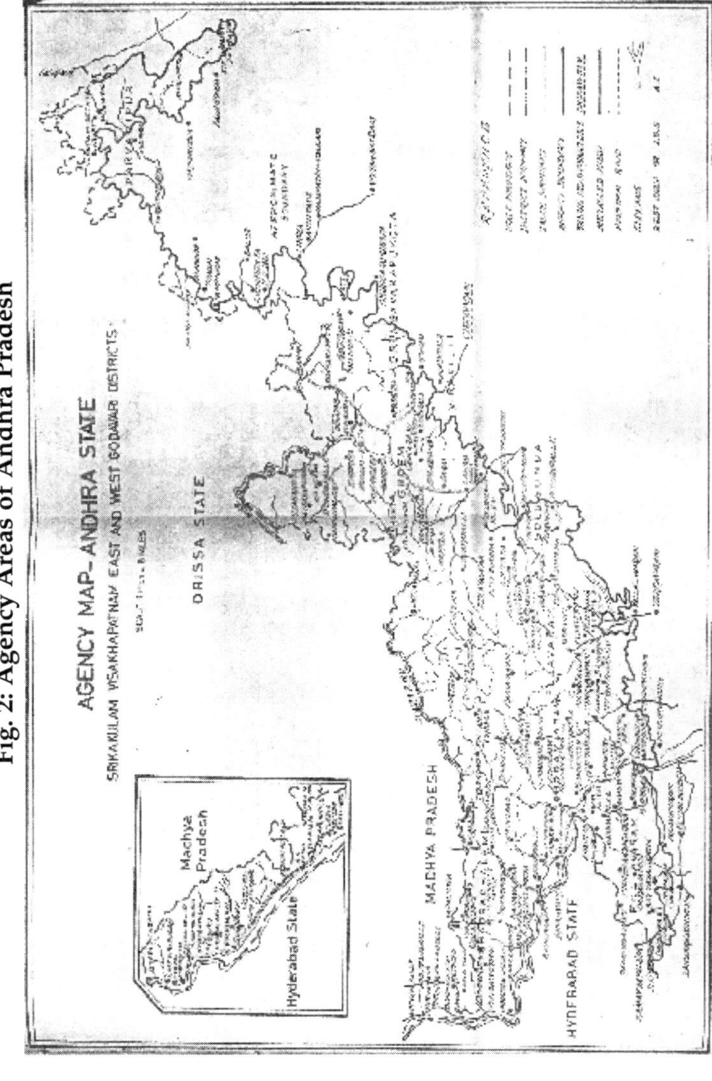

Source: Annexure, Report of R.S. Malayappan, 1951.

problem with the Scheduled Districts Act XIV, 1874 aiming to protect tribals from the danger of further land alienation and indebtedness. Exercising the power under Section 6 of the Scheduled Districts Act 1874, the local government issued rules for the administration of the Agency Tracts and for regulation of the procedure to be adopted by the Officers to administer them. Subsequently, the Agency Tracts Interest and Land Transfer Act 1917 (Act of 1917) was passed limiting the rate of interest and to check the transfer of land in the Agency Tracts in Ganjam, Vizagapatnam and Godavari Districts. By a subsequent notification, the Act was extended to the taluk of Bhadrachalam in the East Godavari District.

Under Section 2 of the Act, Agency Tracts were defined to mean Scheduled Districts, as defined in the Acts XIV and XV of 1874. The ineffective implementation of protective legislations triggered movements in the tribal belt. Thus the Lagarayi *fituri* began with a string of dacoities by a Koya-Kammaras, but the sympathies of at least one muttadar was involved; in February 1917, Mottadam Virayya Dora, *muttadar* of Gudem Patavidi, was deported to Visakhapatnam for complicity in the uprising. This establishes that the Act 1917 was introduced due to this revolt.

By the Agency Land and Interest Act of 1917, the Government of Madras made a belated attempt to protect the hill men from indebtedness and land alienation. The Act prohibited contracts in which the rate of interest would exceed 24 per cent per year and forbade any transfer of immovable property in the Agency Tracts from a hill man to an outsider without the Agent's prior consent. The bill was strongly opposed by the Indian Members of the Madras Legislative Council who threw back at the British their own shibboleths of 'progress' and 'development'. The District Association of Visakhapatnam, a forerunner of the District Congress Committee, urged that the eighty year only distinction between the administrations of the Agency and the plains should be scrapped and free immigration into the hills be permitted. They claimed that contact with the plains' cultivators had already proved beneficial to the hill men through the introduction of improved methods of agriculture.[97]

The 1918 Montagu and Chelmsford Report suggested that the backward area where the primitive people or tribals live should be excluded from the proposed political reform and the administration entrusted to the Governors of the provinces. Subsequently, the Government of India Act 1919 under Section 52 A and finally under the more stringent provisions of the Government of India Act of 1935 incorporated the tribal areas into two parts: 'wholly excluded and partially excluded areas' for their special treatment.[98]

The partially excluded areas comprised the East Godavari Agency, the Polavaram *taluk* of the West Godavari Agency. The tribes inhabiting these tracts are the Koya, Koya Dora and Hill Reddy. They largely practise *podu* cultivation. Crime is scarce and life was simple. The mechanism of justice followed therefore needs to be simple.[99]

The Simon Commission Report highlighted the twin dangers the tribal and hill people faced when exposed to the general laws: the risk of their agricultural land passing to more well-equipped and informed section of the population and the likely risk of them getting trapped by moneylenders. The Government of India Act 1935,[100] dealt with excluded and partially excluded areas (classification of Scheduled Districts) and the administration was exclusively vested in the Governor of the Province. The Government of India (adoption of Indian laws) Order, 1937 repealed the 1874 Act

97. Arnold, David. Memorial from Sec. Dist. Assoc., Vishakhapatnam, to Sec., Local and Municipal, November 8, 1916, L/P&J/6/408 cited in Ranjit Guha (Ed.) Rebellious Hillmen: 1839-1924 in *Subaltern Studies*, OUP, Delhi, 1986.
98. For details see Ghurye, G.S. *The Scheduled Tribes*, pp. 70-97.
99. Report of the Excluded and Partially Excluded Areas Sub-Committee (A.V. Thakkar Committee), August 18, 1947.
100. Based on The Simon Commission Report.

and brought excluded and partially excluded areas directly under the governance of the Governor.

While alienation of revenue land among tribals was acknowledged during the colonial rule, the right of tribals residing in the forest areas without any legally valid documentary evidence was historically never acknowledged. The loss of tribal control over land, both revenue and forest, was the principal reason for several tribal rebellions starting from the late 18th century through the 19th century, to the first few decades of the 20th century. Some of these tribal revolts were localized, while the others were more widespread. These rebellions focused and asserted the traditionally inalienable rights of the tribals on the local resources, land and forests. The imperialists as a colonial power created a new *zamindari* and other feudal systems as the *mutta* system, *mahals* and *mokasa* in the tribal areas of Andhra Pradesh. These systems were historical off-shoots of feudal landlordism. The imperialists in the pre-independence period encouraged the classes from outside tribal areas to exploit and forcibly bring tribal land resources into their personal ownership and control. The Adivasis expressed their dissent and protest in various forms against such feudal landlords.

The condition of the tribal population improved considerably as a result of the Rampa Rebellion. The various orders passed from time to time with the view of ameliorating the conditions of the tribal population of the East Godavari Agency were ultimately consolidated in a legislation known as the Agency Tracts Interest and Land Transfer Act of 1917. Similar to the position of tribals in the British Presidency, the tribals in Telangana Districts of the Nizam's rule in the State of Hyderabad suffered at the hands of land grabbers, landlords, unscrupulous traders and moneylenders. Whenever tanks were constructed or renovated during the Nizam's period, the non-tribals came to these tribal areas as contractors and started grabbing the land of the tribals by making a transit stay. Some of the non-tribal labourers too settled as peasants, turning the tribal peasants into landless labourers. In short, the initiation or resumption of the state's activity in the areas of excise, forest and revenue resulted in non-tribal immigration to the tribal areas and alienation of tribal land. Imposing heavy taxes on tribals and forcing them to retreat deep into the forest may be another reason for the rebellion.[101]

By the late 1930s, the tribals of Adilabad District were subjected to a dual onslaught, one by the non-tribals who encroached on their agricultural land and the other by the forest officials who expanded the boundaries of the reserved forest at the expense of their traditional habitat. The resultant conflict culminated in the death of ten Gonds in a police firing in the 1940s.[102] The tribals in Adilabad district rebelled in 1940 under the leadership of the tribal, Komram Bhim following alienation of tribal land and forest reservation rules. The non-tribal settlers managed to obtain title deeds for the occupied land which once belonged to the tribals. A large chunk of land which had been cultivated on Sivai Jamabandhi tenure (government land encroachments) and lying fallow at the time of demarcation was included in the Reserve. The policy of clearing large tracts of forest of all human habitations including the old, established villages inhabited for many generations led to armed resistance. Prof. Haimendorf, the Austrian born English anthropologist, was invited by the Nizam's Government to study the reasons for the unrest among the tribals.

The struggle ultimately resulted in the promulgation of the Tribal Areas Regulation 1356 Fasli (1946 A.D). This Regulation empowered the government to make rules for improved administration of any notified tribal area in respect of the tribals and of their relations with non-tribals. The substance of this regulation was incorporated in the Tribal

101. Haimendorf, C. von Furer. *Tribes of India: The Struggle for Survival*, Oxford University Press, New Delhi, 1985.
102. Reddy, Subba N. (1988), op. cit.

Areas Regulation 1359 Fasli (1949 AD) and the rules giving effect to its provisions were issued by the Revenue Department as Notified Tribal Area Rules 1359 Fasli on November 16, 1949.

The most important provision of this Regulation was that no court of law or revenue authority had any jurisdiction in any Notified Tribal Area in any dispute relating to land, house or house site occupied, claimed, rented or possessed by any tribal or from which any tribal may have been evicted whether by process of law or otherwise, during a period of one year preceding the notification of such an area as a Notified Tribal Area.

In contrast, in the adjoining provinces of British India, the Government of Hyderabad State had not provided any special privileges for tribal communities till 1946.

2.5.2 *Post-Independence Period*

In 1950, certain areas in the Andhra and Telengana region were notified as Scheduled Areas by Presidential orders. Exercising the powers of the Governor under the Fifth Schedule, viz. to make regulation for the peace and good governance of the Scheduled Area after consulting the Tribes Advisory Council, the Governor issued the Andhra Pradesh Scheduled Area Land Transfer Regulation, 1959 (Regulation 1 of 1959). This came into force on March 4, 1959, partially repealing the earlier Agency Tracts Land Transfer Act of 1917. This was to regulate the transfer of land in the Scheduled Areas of East Godavari, West Godavari, Visakhapatnam and Srikakulam. The Tribal Area Regulation 1359 Fasali (1949) in the Telangana districts was repealed in 1963 and got replaced by the Andhra Pradesh Scheduled Area Land Transfer Regulations 1 of 59 which came into force on December 1, 1963. As a result, the Andhra Pradesh Scheduled Areas Land Transfer Regulation, 1959 was made applicable to the areas in the districts of Adilabad, Warangal, Khammam and Mahbubnagar as well. The regulation states that, notwithstanding anything contained in any enactment, rule of law in force in the Agency Tracts, any transfer of immovable property in the Agency Tracts by a member of a ST, shall be absolutely null and void unless made:

(i) in favour of any other member of a Scheduled Tribe or a registered society as defined in clause (f) of Section 2 of the Madras Cooperative Societies Act, 1932 (Madras Act VL of 1932), composed solely of members of the STs, or

(ii) with the previous sanction of the State Government, or subject to rules made in this behalf, with the previous consent of the Agent or of any prescribed officer in writing.

The excessive exploitative conditions induced by external interventions, the ineffectiveness of the government response in prevention of ST land alienation and restoration of alienated ST land and the ineffective legislations triggered the Naxalite movement in Srikakulam region between 1968-70. The peasant uprising in Naxalbari in Darjeeling district of West Bengal[103] prompted the tribals of the Srikakulam District to resort to armed struggle in October 1968. The Naxalite movement was not confined only to Srikakulam District, but spread quickly to other areas of the state as well, particularly to Warangal and Khammam Districts.[104] All the uprisings were defensive movements against state oppression. They were the last resort of the tribals driven to despair by the encroachments of outsiders on their land. The Srikakulam Naxalite movement again drew the attention of the State. The State then felt that: 'It would be absolutely necessary to create conditions for peace and maintain peace and prevent the new non-tribals from settling down in the Scheduled Area. If the alienations are permitted to the non-

103. During May-July 1967.

104. Parthasarathy, et al. *Peasant Movements and Changing Agrarian Structure in AP*, Department of Cooperation and Applied Economics, Andhra University, Visakhapatnam (mimeo), 1979.

tribals there is a danger of large-scale exploitation by the new non-tribals again with the result peace will be disturbed in that area.'

With a view to maintain peace and to govern the area effectively, Regulation 1 of 1970 was passed by the Andhra Pradesh Governor. A non-ST who validly acquired the land title was not to be disturbed, but he would not be allowed to sell his land to a non-ST which could be a new entrant to the area. This was to ensure that the land of STs should not be frittered away to outsiders through transfer and that non-STs should not be allowed to infiltrate into the Scheduled Areas by getting allotments of land made in their favour. When such transactions take place, the government was to restore land to the tribal or his heirs, after evicting the non-ST. Unless new entrants into the Scheduled Areas were prevented from settling down in the Scheduled Areas by purchasing properties either from STs or non-STs, it was not possible to prevent the exploitation of STs. Regulation 1 of 1970 was passed to enforce the valid provisions of Regulation 1 of 1959. This was to restrict or prohibit the alienation of non-ST land to other non-STs. The Regulations 1 of 70 prohibits any transfer of immovable property in the Agency Tracts to a non-ST person. However, it permits transfer of land to an ST or a society registered or deemed to be registered under the Andhra Pradesh Cooperative Societies Act, 1964 (Act 7 of 1964) which is composed solely of members of the STs. This is based on the presumption that any immovable property in the Agency Tracts in the possession of a non-ST is acquired by him or his predecessor through a transfer made to him by an ST unless the contrary is proved.

When a person intending to sell one's land is not able to affect such sale, due to the fact that no ST is willing to purchase the land on the terms offered, then the person may apply to the Agent, the Agency Divisional Officer or any other prescribed officer for the acquisition of such land by the State Government. The Agent, Agency Divisional Officer or any other prescribed officer may take over such land on payment of compensation in accordance with Section 10 of the Andhra Pradesh Ceiling on Agricultural Holdings Act, 1961 (Act X of 1961). This land vests with the State Government free from all encumbrances and is to be disposed of in favour of STs or a society registered or deemed to be registered under the Andhra Pradesh Cooperative Societies Act, 1964 composed solely of members of the STs.

If a transfer of immovable property is made in contravention of sub-section (1), the Agent, the Agency Divisional Officer or any other prescribed Officer may, on application by anyone interested, or on information given in writing by a public servant, or *suo motu* decree ejectment of those in possession of the property, after due notice to him, and may restore it to the transferor or his heirs. If the transferor or his heirs are not willing to take back the property or where their whereabouts are not known, the Agent, the Agency Divisional Officer or the prescribed officer may order the assignment or sale of the property to any other ST member or a society registered or deemed to be registered under any law relating to Cooperative Societies in the State composed solely of members of the STs, or otherwise dispose of it, as if it was property at the disposal of the State Government.

By further amendment to the Regulation, Section 6-A and 6-B were incorporated, making any acquisition of the immovable property in the Scheduled Areas by non-STs in contravention of Land Transfer Regulations 1 of 59, as amended by 1 of 70 or continuing in possession of such property after a decree of ejectment is passed, as a cognizable offence. Andhra Pradesh has an exemplary Land Transfer Regulations 1 of 70. Despite such a strong legislation there are a large number of pending cases where land remains to be restored to STs.[105] The legal provisions have been inadequate in tackling the problem in all its dimensions and

105. Swaminadhan, D. Draft Policy Paper, Tribal Welfare and Development, GoI, Delhi, 2004.

the implementation process has been weak so as to render them ineffective.[106]

The suo motu power given to the government to proceed against non-STs without waiting for a complaint from an ST seems to be an ideal arrangement, but in the given administrative culture, it has been more of a boon to the non-STs than to STs. In proceedings taken up suo motu by the government, the non-ST faces only the government. The government does not take the trouble of finding out who among the local tribals may have a claim to the land. It does not publicise the enquiry in the village. The officer hearing the cases, designated as Special Deputy Collector, merely looks into the documents provided by the non-ST, and if they appear reliable, he approves the right of the non-ST over the land.[107]

In practice, the orders being issued in favour of STs are also not being implemented by the enforcing authorities. Unsuccessful non-ST parties continue their possession and enjoyment of land. As on October 31, 2005, the detected cases of non-ST encroachments were about 70,000 which involved about 3,15,000 acres of land. Of this, only about one lakh acres were restored to STs, 35 years after the promulgation of the regulation. Over two lakh acres of disputed land are still in possession of non-STs. The stark reality that stares one in the face is that about 50 per cent of the cultivable land in the Scheduled Areas of Andhra Pradesh is under the occupation of the non-STs.[108]

As many of the newcomers were able to occupy cultivable lands, there can be no doubt that the minor revenue officials, and in particular the *patwari* and the revenue inspectors, were

106. Karuppaiyan, E. Alienation of Tribal Land in Tamil Nadu, *Economic and Political Weekly*, June 2, 1990, p. 1185.
107. Balagopal, K. Land Unrest in Andhra Pradesh–III – Illegal Acquisition in Tribal Areas, *Economic and Political Weekly*, October 6, 2007, p. 4031.
108. Reddy, Subba N. (2006), op. cit.

won over by them as many were wealthy enough to pay large bribes to corrupt officials. The laws prohibiting the acquisition of tribal land by the non-STs were obviously ignored. Otherwise, it would have been impossible for the recent migrants with no claim to ST status, to acquire house sites and arable land at the expense of the Gond tribals who lost all or most of their land within a span of a few years.[109]

Of 76,762 cases covering an extent of 3,39,699 acres of land, 74,973 cases covering an extent of 3,32,852 acres were disposed of by the SDC Courts by the end of January 2010. The courts decided 36,512 cases of an extent of 1,43,683 acres of land in favour of the STs. However, the enforcement machinery set up under the Regulations could only restore 1,22,011 acres of land pertaining to the 30,905 cases out of a total of 36,512. On the contrary, the non-STs were able to secure orders in their favour in 38,461 cases and retained 1,89,169 acres of land in their possession.

Table 5 shows that the success rate for land acquisition is 49 per cent in the case of tribals, and 51 per cent in the case of non-STs. STs were able to regain land possession from non-STs only to the extent of 43 per cent of the total extent of land, covered by cases disposed of, while the non-ST could retain 57 per cent of the disputed land. Due to the failure of the implementing machinery in implementing the orders passed by the SDC Court in favour of STs, only 85 per cent of the total cases were disposed of in favour of STs, and only 85 per cent of land extent was physically handed over to them. This shows the failure of the administrative machinery in executing orders passed by the court in favour of STs. The non-STs continued to possess land even when the eviction orders were passed against them.

The Scheduled Area is to ensure justice to STs, their survival and livelihood. But as K. Balagopal pointed out:

> It is not enough if a disadvantaged class of people are endowed with legal rights. Legal instruments created for the benefit of

109. Haimendorf, C. von Furer (1985), op. cit.

Table 5: Outcome of Cases under LTR at SDC Courts as on January 31, 2010

Sl. No.	*District*	*Cases Detected*		*Cases Disposed*		*Cases Decided in Favour of STs*		*Cases Decided in Favour of Non-STs*		*Land Restored to Tribals*		*Balance Cases at the End of the Month (col. 3-5 & 4-6)*	
		Nos.	*Extent (Acres)*	*Nos.*	*Extent (Acres)*	*Nos.*	*Extent (Acres)*	*Nos.*	*Extent (Acres)*	*Nos.*	*Extent (Acres)*	*Nos.*	*Extent (Acres)*
	1.	2.	3.	4.	5.	6.	7.	8.	9.	10.	11.	12.	13.
1.	Srikakulam	462	1100	**453**	**1024**	296	538	157	486	250	522	**9**	**76**
2.	Vizianagaram	1364	7544	**1343**	**7501**	955	5631	388	1870	850	5498	**21**	**43**
3.	Visakhapatnam	5708	22731	**5480**	**22087**	4359	17721	1121	4366	3029	13944	**228**	**644**
4.	East Godavari	8485	49637	**8264**	**48768**	3751	19667	4513	29101	3392	17685	**221**	**869**
5.	West Godavari	11611	62121	**11477**	**60820**	2584	11082	8893	49738	2451	10081	**134**	**1301**
6.	Khammam	33582	126713	**33325**	**125834**	15514	52192	17811	73642	12750	41662	**257**	**879**
7.	Warangal	7289	15784	**7052**	**15218**	4865	8964	2187	6254	4865	8964	**237**	**566**
8.	Adilabad	8245	54008	**7564**	**51543**	4175	27839	3389	23704	3305	23606	**681**	**2465**
9.	Mahbubnagar	16	61	**15**	**57**	13	49	2	8	13	49	**1**	**4**
	Total:	**76762**	**339699**	**74973**	**332852**	**36512**	**143683**	**38461**	**189169**	**30905**	**122011**	**1789**	**6847**

Source: Office of the Commissioner of Tribal Welfare, Hyderabad, Administration Report, January 2010.

the socially privileged can be expected to find their way to implementation without anything else. This is not the case with legal rights enacted for the benefit of the disadvantaged.[110]

2.6 Review of Judicial Interventions

The concept of land as a commodity comes into conflict with the tradition of common property among communities, such as STs who have had no documented system of land ownership and hence, are unable to provide this particular proof of ownership to claim compensation in case of displacement. The courts never consider this ground reality in dispensation of justice in the tribal land cases. The land is their most important natural, valuable asset and imperishable endowment from which the STs derive their sustenance, social status, dignity, economic and social equality, permanent place of abode, work and living. It is a source of security and economic empowerment. Therefore, the tribal peoples have great emotional attachment to their land. It provides a means of economic empowerment in social democracy.[111]

The Supreme Court in the P. Ramireddy vs. State of Andhra Pradesh (AIR 1988 SC 1626) held that the provisions of the Andhra Pradesh Scheduled Area Land Transfer Regulations 1 of 70 are constitutionally valid. A legislation, which in essence and substance aims at restoration of land to the 'tribals' that originally belonged to them but which passed into the hands of 'non-tribals', certainly cannot be characterized as unreasonable. True, transfer by 'non-tribals' to 'non-tribals' would not diminish the pool. As a matter of fact, it would be unjust, unfair and highly unreasonable

---

110. Balagopal, K. Foreword to book *Land Rights of Adivasis* by P. Trinadha Rao (2004) Laya Publications, Visakhapatnam.
111. Samata Appellants vs. State of Andhra Pradesh & Others with Ms. Hyderabad Abrasives & Minerals (P) Ltd. (appellant) & State of Andhra Pradesh & Others, Respondents. AIR 1997 Supreme Court 3297.

merely to freeze the situation, instead of reversing the injustice and restoring the status-quo-ante.[112]

The term 'transfer' under Land Transfer Regulation means mortgage with or without possession, lease, sale, gift, exchange or any other deal with immovable property. It should not be a testamentary disposition and includes a charge on such property or a contract relating to such property in respect of such mortgage, lease, sale, gift, exchange or other dealings. This means land transfers through execution of a 'will' by a testator are not covered by the word 'transfer' under the Land Transfer Regulations. However, the interpretation of the word 'transfer' by the High Court of Andhra Pradesh, keeping in view of the expression 'dealing with immoveable property', includes acts of 'forcible dispossession and encroachment'. Thus a dispossessed ST is entitled to restoration of possession of his land.[113] The word 'other dealing' in the Regulation also includes allotment of shops at bus stands in Agency Areas by means of tenders and in the form of licences. The word 'licence' can be read under the general expression 'other dealings' used in Section 2(g) of the Regulation. Hence, even permitting non-ST commercial establishments by the State is banned under the Regulation.[114] The Supreme Court, while dealing with a case under Orissa Scheduled Areas Transfer of Immovable Property (by Scheduled Tribes) Regulation (2 of 1956), held that the expression 'transfer' in 'Transfer of immovable property' by STs includes any 'dealing' with such property. The word 'deal with' is not defined in the Statute. Its dictionary meaning, taken as safe guide, can be extended to achieve the legislative object of the Act: transaction or dealing with immovable property having effect of extinguishing title

112. P. Rami Reddy & Others vs. State of AP & Another. (1988) 22 Reports (SC) 364.
113. M. Suresh Bhargava & Another vs. State of AP & Others.1989 (2) ALT 516.
114. Adarsha Adivasi Mahila Samithi & Others vs. Agent to the Government Khammam & Others. 2003 (5) ALD 284.

of a member of aboriginal tribe and vesting the same with the non-ST. This can be construed as 'transfer of immovable property.'[115]

Further, the word 'exchange' in the definition of 'transfer' also includes exchange of shared immovable property among family members in the Scheduled Areas. Partition of family property is permitted but not exchange of property during the division of inherited family property by non-STs.[116] The High Court of Andhra Pradesh further held that the word 'transfer' includes 'contract to sell'.[117] The High Court also held that even if the land classified as *Gayalu* or government *poramboke*, the person who is in possession of such land, must be said to be dealing with such immovable property. Therefore, the same falls within the scope of 'transfer' as defined under Section 2(g) of the Regulation.[118]

The Supreme Court held that the word 'person' in Section 3(1) would include natural persons as well as juristic persons, and the Government. The word 'person' would be so interpreted as to include State or juristic person, and corporate bodies. Transfer of land by juristic persons or allotment of land by State to non-STs, is thus prohibited. This ruling restricts the power of the government to grant lease to non-STs in Agency Areas for mining or any other such purposes. The Constitution of India under Article 21 guarantees 'Right to life'. Right to life means far more than mere survival. Thus, STs have the fundamental right to social and economic empowerment.[119]

---

115. Amrendra Prapat Singh, Appellant vs. Tej Bahadur Prajapati and others, AIR 2004 Supreme Court 3782
116. Ashok Vs. Baba Rao and Another. 2002(6)ALT 296.
117. Kakarla Nageswara Rao and other vs Government of AP rep. by its Secretary (Tribal Welfare) Departtment, Hyderabad. 1995(3) ALT 164.
118. Vuppuluri Veera Venkata Raju and Others vs. Special Deputy Tahsildar, Tribal Welfare, Gangavaram (V&M), E.G. District and Others. 2007 (6) ALD 292.
119. Samata Appellants vs. State of Andhra Pradesh & Others, (1997), op. cit.

The legal presumption in the law and further objective of the provision has had a trace in the argument of the report of the Schedule Areas and Schedule Tribes Commission (Dhebar Commission) in 1961. The Dhebar Commission recommended that 'all surrenders (of tribal land) must be only to the State, which should hold the surrendered land as trustee for the tribals.' Once it is understood that the state is not the owner but a trustee under legal duty to protect the natural resources, the state sovereign would be precluded from taking the possession of the land without the owner's consent, the consent being a free and informed one. The customary rights of STs are often not recognized and thus those who depended on such resources were not considered eligible for compensation.

The laws made applicable to the Scheduled Areas indicate an anxiety to safeguard the interests of tribals and to ensure that the land in the Scheduled Areas should remain in the possession of the STs. The High Court of Andhra Pradesh held that the object seems to be that all immovable property in Agency Tracts, which was held by STs at one time, as far as possible, must be restored back to them. Therefore, a non-ST transferor, after the commencement of Land Transfer Regulations 1 of 70, cannot seek restoration of the alienated land to another non-ST; nor can the non-ST transferee claim retention of the land.[120]

Governments, from time to time, issued several orders for protecting the non-STs' landed interest in the Scheduled Areas, even after the Regulation 1 of 70 was promulgated by the Governor under the Fifth Schedule of the Constitution due to political pressures. One such was G.O MS 129 dated August 13, 1979 directing the officers concerned not to evict non–ST landless poor in occupation of government land in Scheduled Areas up to an extent of 5 acres of wet land or 10

120. Vemana Somalamma & Another (Appl), Veera Sunkar Deo & Another (pet) vs. Deputy Collector (TW), Rampachodavaram, E.G. Dist, 1993(1) ALT 409 (FB).

acres of dry land. This G.O. was questioned before the High Court and quashed in 1984 as illegal and without jurisdiction.[121]

The subsequent G.O 41 in 1971 and G.O 951 in 1974 prohibiting eviction of non-ST Sivai Zamadars in occupation of government land in Scheduled Areas up to an extent of 2.5 acres wet or 5 acres dry land if they are in continuous possession of those land for a period of not less than 10 years, and preventing eviction of Sivai Zamdars belonging to the Scheduled Castes in occupation of government land up to an extent of 2.5 acres wet and 5 acres of dry land, if they are in occupation of the land since 1969, were all quashed as they are against the provisions of Regulation 1 of 70.[122] The High Court held that the land situated in the Scheduled Areas cannot be acquired under the Land Acquisition Act for providing house-sites even to Scheduled Castes *de hors* the Regulation.[123] The Land Transfer Regulation as amended by the Regulation 1 of 1970 prevails over the provisions of Regulation 2 of 1970 and no *ryotwari patta* can be granted in violation of the provisions of Regulation 1 of 1970. Such a *patta* would not bind the authorities under Regulation 1 of 1970.[124]

The main purpose of the Andhra Pradesh Scheduled Area Land Transfer Regulations 1 of 59 is to invalidate any transfer of land situated in the Agency Tracts in favour of the non-ST. In order to effectuate that intention, the Regulation set up separate machinery. On the other hand, the Ryotwari Settlement Regulation 2 of 70 was enacted to provide for the *ryotwari* settlement of certain land areas in the Scheduled Area of Andhra Pradesh. Section 7 requires that a non-ST

121. AP Girijan Welfare Students and Youth Union vs. State of AP W.P. No. 1755/90 dated December 5, 1984.
122. P. Gangamma vs. Vasudha Misra & Another. 1998(2) ALD 35.
123. Koppula Saramma vs. Government of AP Social Welfare Department & Others. 2001 (3) ALT 501.
124. Gadde Nagabushanamma vs. Government of AP & Others. 1999(5) ALD 430.

shall not be entitled to a *ryotwari patta* if his possession and occupation of the land is void or illegal under the Regulation 1 of 59. The proper way to read these two Regulations is to allow both of them to operate while giving primary importance to the operation of Regulation 1 of 59. Any decision under these Regulations by the authorities in determining rights over lands will prevail over the other laws. It means even a *ryotwari patta* granted to a non-ST against the provisions of Land Transfer Regulations would not give a better land entitlement to him. Thus, any decision made under Regulation 2 of 1970 can only be tentative and provisional, and would be subject to the decision made under the Regulation 1 of 59.[125] The Land Transfer Regulations are superior and legally binding on the other legislations. The Supreme Court held that the prohibition against transfer and declaration of nullity enjoined under the Amended Land Transfer Regulation having been held to be an emanation of Para 5(2) of the Fifth Schedule to the Constitution itself. The determination of invalidity declared under the provisions of Land Transfer Regulations will have to be held as overriding any contrary determination under any other Regulation.[126]

Even the High Court was not inclined to apply the principle of *res judicata*[127] to the tribal land alienation cases under the Regulations, and give a restrictive frame for its application in tribal land cases. It was held that orders passed in the first proceedings initiated under the Regulation will not operate as *res judicata* if the later proceedings are initiated by a third party or by the same party on the basis of any further material.[128] It was further held that the earlier

125. Kandula Brahmaiah vs. The Deputy Collector (Tribal Welfare) Rampachodavaram, E.G. Dist. W.P. 2169/1981 dated December 10, 1986-unreported.
126. Samatha vs. State of AP (AIR 1997 SC 3297.)
127. Meaning a matter already judged.
128. N. Durga Rao & Another vs. Special Deputy Collector (TW) Kota Ramachandrapuram W.G. Dist. & Others. 2003(6) ALD (NOC) 68.

proceedings of a case do not operate as *res judicata* in the present proceedings if the land question involved in the earlier proceedings is distinct and different from the one on the basis of which the present proceedings are initiated.[129]

The mere fact that on the earlier occasion a petition filed under the Land Transfer Regulation 1959 was dismissed, does not confer any right on the non-ST so long as the statutory order subsists, viz. the void sale subsists. The statute prescribes that any transaction entered into between an ST and non-ST or between a non-ST and a non-ST, are void per se.[130]

However, judicial activism has put an obstacle to the very objective of Land Transfer Regulations. The Supreme Court of India held that the Andhra Pradesh Scheduled Areas Land Transfer Regulation (1 of 1959), Section 3 (as it stood before and after amendment in 1963 and 1970), prohibits transfer of immovable properties in the Scheduled Area prospectively. This means the Regulations do not adversely affect completed transactions of transfer which have taken place before the enforcement of Regulations.[131]

Dealing with a tribal land question situated in the Telangana area, the High Court applied the same principle and held that authorities acting under the said Regulation cannot interfere with the alienations effected before the commencement of the Regulation 1 of 1970. If the said transactions are illegal in view of any other provisions of law, it is for the appropriate forum to take action, but they cannot be declared void by the Deputy Collector acting under

---

129. Special Deputy Collector (TW), Rampachodavaram, E.G. District & Others vs. Datla Venkapathi Raju & Others. 2003 (1) ALD 386. (D.B.) A similar view was taken by the court in G. Nageswararao & China Nageswararao vs. Government of AP and Others. 2007 (6) ALD 621.
130. Ch. Satyanarayana vs. The Agent to Government & District Collector Visakhapatnam, W.P. 6065/1979-unreported.
131. Deputy Collector vs. Venkata Ramanaiah & Another-AIR 1996 S.C. 224.

Section 3 of Regulation 1 of 1970. The High Court held that the authorities under the Regulation, while admitting the transfer to be prior to December 1, 1963, cannot set aside the same on the ground that it was by an unregistered sale deed and therefore not valid. There is no jurisdiction or power conferred on the authority to question the validity of alienation otherwise than being in contravention of the regulation.[132] Therefore, these rulings have given a wider scope to non-STs to escape from the clutches of tribal protective land laws, and manipulation of pre-dated unregistered agreements and sale deeds.

The TAC, in its meetings held in 1984, recommended giving retrospective effect to the Land Transfer Regulations 1 of 59 from 1917 in the Andhra Region and in the Telangana Region from 1949. But the governments did not accept the decision of the TAC as it would affect their non-ST vote bank in the Scheduled Areas.

The rulings of Courts further weakened the unwilling state in enforcing the Land Transfer Regulations. The Regulations provided *suo moto* power to initiate proceedings against the non-ST occupants in the Scheduled Areas. However, the rulings of the Court limited its power affecting the tribal land rights. The High Court of Andhra Pradesh held that exercising a *suo motu* power after a lapse of reasonable time would be arbitrary and contrary to the principle of 'rule of law' enshrined in the Constitution and exercising such a *suo moto* power after 14 or 15 years would be *ipso facto* unreasonable.[133]

Adivasis used to settle their land disputes only through customary law before the introduction of the English common law which became the sole legitimate recourse for enforcing of land rights. Predictably, the usual difficulties

---

132. K. Mahalaxmi & Another vs. Government of Andhra Pradesh & Others. 2000 (5) ALD 588

133. Kola Mahalaxmi vs. Agent to Government, Khammam & Others. 1999(6) ALD 718.

with any *imposed* law—prolonged procedures, impractical rules of evidence, and delays in disposal of cases—hinder a verdict even in the simplest of cases. The Adivasis give more value to oral rather than documentary evidence. However, the Indian Evidence Act gives more weightage to documentary evidence which is known to the non-ST parties involved in the land issue and they have managed to document the land records favourably to gain advantage during court enquiries. Further, there is no scope for quick justice through established courts for settlement of cases. The courts usually take a longer period to pass judgements because the legal procedure is very cumbersome. In this backdrop some of the STs perhaps prefer other forums which could settle their issues. Naxalites could be one among such forums. Adivasis therefore prefer the swift justice delivered by radical groups such as the Naxalites and Maoists flourishing in the hinterland over the procrastinated conventional court system to which they are unaccustomed. They thus become ready recruits for groups as the Maoists who promise protection of the STs' natural rights in return for material and political support.[134]

2.7 Forest Land Rights Deprivation Among Tribals

The evolution of forest laws and policy in India has progressively curtailed the rights of STs for sustenance and livelihood derived from the forests. The access of STs to forests and common property resources has been declining due to the progressive abrogation of their rights, largely by the state itself.

Andhra Pradesh is the fifth largest state in terms of geographical area and the third largest state in terms of forest cover in the country. The state is a distinct geographical entity occupying the east central plateau of India with a long

134. See A Spectre Haunting India, *The Economist*, August 17, 2006, online: <http://www.economist.com/world/asia/displaystory.cfm?story_id=7799247>.

coastline. Of the 2,75,068 sq.kms of geographical area, forests occupy 63,813 sq.kms of land. Rich in flora and fauna, the forests exhibit a wide range of types in composition and ecological status. About 3,695 Gram Panchayats in the state of Andhra Pradesh have forest interface covered by 20,32,303 acres of land as per the Report of the Tribal Welfare Department (2007).

There are 50.24 lakh STs in the State as per the 2001 Census of which about 60 per cent live in Scheduled Areas. 62 per cent of the Scheduled Area in the state is covered by reserve forests and more than 60 per cent of reserve forests in the state are located in the Scheduled Areas which confirm that STs and forests are closely interlinked.

Table 6: Forest Laws Applicable to Andhra Pradesh

S.No.	*Short Title or Subject*	*Year*
1	Indian Forest Act	1865
2	Revised Indian Forest Act (Act VII of 1878)	1878
3	Indian Forest Act	1927
4	Madras Forest Act (Andhra Area)	1882
5	Forest Act for Hyderabad State	1900
6	Revised Forest Act for Hyderabad State	1916
7	Hyderabad Forest Act	1945
8	AP Forest Act (Integration of Madras and Hyderabad Forest Acts)	1967
9	Andhra Pradesh Minor Forest Produce (Regulations of Trade) Act	1971
10	The AP Scheduled Areas Minor Forest Produce (Regulation of Trade)	1979
11	The Forest (Conservation) Act	1980
12	The AP Scheduled Area Minor Forest Produce (Regulation of Trade) Rules	1990
13	The Scheduled Tribes and Other Traditional Forest Dwellers (Recognition of Forest Rights) Act	2006

In Hyderabad State, the forests were considered subservient to the interest of agriculture and were consequently administered by the district officials. A separate Forest Department was created in 1867 to protect exclusively certain plant species under a simple set of rules. The rest of the general forest produce and administration remained with the district officials. The revenue officials permitted cultivation in the forests. This system was considered unsatisfactory and the government took steps to gain control over the communities. In 1893, the government declared vast tracts covered by forest growth as protected forests and placed them under the sole charge of the Forest Department. To have legal control over forests, a Forest Act was enacted in 1900. Subsequently, it was revised and the Forest Act of 1916 was brought in. This Act, based on the lines of the Indian Forest Act 1927, was repealed by the Hyderabad Forest Act 1945. The Madras Presidency formulated its own Act, viz. the Madras Forest Act 1882.

When the State of Andhra Pradesh was formed on November 1, 1956, the laws in force then continued to be in force by virtue of the States Reorganization Act 1956. Later, the Andhra Pradesh (Andhra Area) Forest Act 1882 (or Madras Forest Act 1882), and the Andhra Pradesh (Telangana Area) Forest Act 1945 (or Hyderabad Forest Act 1945), were integrated and the Andhra Pradesh Forest Act 1967 was enacted for the protection and management of forests in Andhra Pradesh. The Act empowers the state to constitute any land as a reserve forest and Forest Settlement Officers were appointed to determine the right of the local communities over such land. Each of these legislations has a distinct purpose. Thus, the Andhra Pradesh Forest Act is a consolidated legislation for all purposes, including forest management and conservation of forests, in Andhra Pradesh.

The 1972 Report of the Task Force on Development of Tribal Areas suggests that: '... customary rights of tribals in land and forests may be recognised. It is inevitable that many of the customary rights of the tribals would require change in course of time for a larger national interest. The specific conditions to be considered are: communal ownership, land settled with the chief on behalf of the community, and individual ownership.'[135]

Chapter III-A (Preservation of Private Forests) of the Andhra Pradesh Forest Act 1967 containing Section 28-A to 28-G was made applicable to the Scheduled Areas in 1977 imposing restrictions on cutting trees in the forest land owned by the communities and empowering the state to prohibit or regulate the removal of trees for any purposes, for the preservation of forests. Further, a notification was issued by the Governor of Andhra Pradesh in 1979 excluding the right to claim *ryotwari patta* over the lands containing trees, shrubs, and coppice growth situated in land tenures of *mutta, mokhasa, zamindari* and other government land. This notification restricted STs to claim Settlement *pattas* over the land in their occupation situated under these land tenures. They are denied rights ensured for seeking Settlement *pattas* under the Ryotwari Settlement Regulations, introduced after abolition of other land tenures as the *mutta, mokhasa, zamindari,* etc. in the Scheduled Areas.

2.8 Revenue and Forest Boundary Disputes

In the Andhra region, villages were surveyed excluding the forest areas. When a reserve forest adjoins the village boundaries, the boundary was demarcated by excluding the forest. However, in the Telangana region, the villages were surveyed including the forests in the villages. The forest blocks may lie in a single or more villages. In tribal areas the villages were initially surveyed to the extent of *patta* land, leaving out vast extents of hilly terrains. Subsequently, the areas between *patta* land of the villages and Reserve Forest land were surveyed and maps prepared. Special survey units for tribal survey under Telugu Grameen Magani Samaradhan were created to survey the Reserve Forest boundaries by a team comprising both the revenue and forest officials with

---

135. Report of the Task Force on Development of Tribal Areas, (Prof. Vidyarthi Committee), April 5, 1972.

reference to the notified forest. The areas lying between Reserve Forest limits and *patta* land of adjacent villages were surveyed to complete a survey of a village in two parts.

In 1987, the government issued a Memo No 26531/87 by the Ministry of Energy, Forests, Environment Science and Technology permitting the assignment of pre-1980 forest land occupations by tribal communities in the reserved forests. Based on this memo, D-Form *pattas* were granted to STs. However, during the implementation of the Joint Forest Management Scheme, the forest department brought such revenue *patta* land under the purview of the scheme and evicted the STs stating that the land is classified as 'forest' in their records. Such instances have been widely evidenced in the tribal areas of East Godavari district.

The conflict between STs and the Forest Department with respect to forest land are not yet settled. A boundary of 21,210 kms remains under dispute and 77,661 acres of land is recorded to be under cultivation by STs in reserve forests before 1980. These are not reguralised yet. This is in addition to recognition of land rights by revenue department in forest areas under Memo No. 26531/87.

Deforestation, mainly due to exploitation of forests for industrial purposes, is yet another manifestation of resource displacement. This has resulted in decreasing access to forest resources by the tribal communities. The non-recognition of customary and traditional rights of STs over the forest land cultivation too is a major concern. STs are often evicted by the Forest Department from their forest land cultivations being labelled as 'encroachers'. Forest land to the extent of 13.43 lakh hectares is under encroachment in the country. In Andhra Pradesh alone 2,95,383 hectares of forest land is recorded as pre-1980 and post-1980 encroachments as on March 31, 2004.[136]

The baseline study conducted by the Integrated Tribal Development Agency in 1991 for the Andhra Pradesh Tribal

---

136. *Parliament Digest, Budget Session*. NCAS Publications, Pune, 2004, p. 53.

Development Project funded by the International Fund for Agricultural Development (IFAD) shows that 62,504 ST households in four northern coastal districts, East Godavari, Visakhapatnam, Vizianagaram and Srikakulam are engaged in shifting cultivation as their only means of survival and livelihood on about 62,948 hectares of land.

There is no regularisation process for these holdings to ensure entitlements in favour of ST occupants. On the other hand, the forest department continues to evict ST occupants of the forest land on the basis of the notification issued long ago. The entire process is contrary to the statement made in the Common Minimum Programme that 'eviction of tribal communities and other forest dwelling communities from forests will be discontinued.'

The World Bank aided projects too are causing displacement of STs who depend on forest land for cultivation. The Forest Department in its Resettlement Action Plan document claims that with the World Bank assisted Andhra Pradesh Forest Project, nearly 37,000 hectares of forests under encroachment in the tribal areas of Visakhapatnam have been voluntarily put under productive tree crops by STs who had encroached upon this land. This statement questions the rehabilitation provided to the displaced STs. This clearly implies that STs have been evicted from land under their occupation of *podu* or shifting cultivation land. This is a clear violation of the World Bank's own policy towards indigenous people (OD4.30, involuntary settlement). Offering a package and using non-government organisations (NGOs) to motivate social capital and compelling STs to move out from the forests land is the hidden agenda of the Forest Department. The state has become an agent to implement the World Bank Projects. NGOs are systematically co-opted by the state. Some of the NGOs act as a curtain to the State and World Bank to hide the displeasure or aggression of the target people. This is to reduce the pressure from the grassroots. This minimizes the demand of STs for regularization of their cultivation in the forest land. The forest department never recognized their rights over land and arbitrarily fixed the reserve forest boundaries in the tribal areas. The conflict between the tribals and forest department in respect of forest land is yet to be settled.

The State has come up with contradictory statements with regard to the extension of the forest land settlements covered by the Scheduled Tribes and Other Traditional Forest Dwellers (Recognition of Forest Rights) Act 2006. The Secretary, Tribal Welfare, Government of Andhra Pradesh, issued guidelines for the implementation of the Act in 2008. The guidelines say that the Forest Department has informed that 2,36,355 hectares of land is under encroachment by forest dwelling STs. This is only an indication and actual settlement of the land will be based on the claims accepted by the District Level Committee. However, according to the reports of the Tribal Welfare Department, Government of Andhra Pradesh, presently 9,93,551 hectares or 24,838,79 acres of land is covered by Preliminary Notification under Section 4 of the Andhra Pradesh Forest Act, 1967. Preliminary Notification refers to a notification issued to the local public informing the intention of the government to declare certain areas as reserved forests. This notification seeks objections from the local people in the reservation process of land as reserve forest. Most of this land has been under preliminary notification for at least the last two decades or even more. Both land and livelihood rights of lakhs of poor people have remained unrecognized on these deemed forests so far. If the rights of the occupants are settled under the Andhra Pradesh Forest Act, it would restrict their rights to lay claim on their possession after the notification is issued.

However, the recent enactment of the Forest Rights Act, 2006, which came into force in 2008, recognizes both the individual and community rights over the forest land. These laws are in addition to the existing rights ensuring land to the Adivasis in the Scheduled Areas. These laws facilitate to seek land entitlements through the recognition of their occupation of forest land. However, the State is interpreting this as distribution of land *pattas* to STs instead of recognising the rights of STs and other forest dwellers over the forest land.

The Forest Rights Act 2006 promises to be a pro-poor institutional reform and indeed, many poor people have already benefited from its implementation. However, the process has been severely anti-poor and so the pro-poor benefits have been restricted in many ways. Surprisingly the government has not distributed titles for community forest land claims but 100 titles were distributed to the Forest Department controlled Vana Samrakshna Samithis (VSS) in Adilabad District.

The Government of Andhra Pradesh granted community forest rights titles to more than 1,669 VSSs for over 9.48 lakh acres of forest lands, by the end of May 2010 instead of Gram Sabha against the letter and spirit of Forest Rights Act as well as PESA. The Ministry of Tribal Affairs, Government of india,[137] held that the grant of Community Forestry Rights (CFR) titles to VSS is illegal and directed the authorities for its withdrawal. The directive is very clear that denial of individual rights and community rights over such VSS areas would also be illegal. However the State Government is dilly-dallying in nullifying the CFR titles granted in favour of VSSs.

Of the total 3,50,146 individual claims received covering an extent of 10,18,828 acres, forest land *pattas* (47%) were distributed to 165,996 individuals covering an extent of 47,3092 acres (46.43%). In respect of community forest rights, 10,965 applications covering an extent of 12,79,206 acres were received, of which 2,106 community forest rights titles were distributed covering an extent of 9,79,207 acres by December 3, 2012 according to the Tribal Welfare Department reports. Among the CFR titles, only 437 were distributed to community covering the extent of around 31,000. The rest

137. Ref: Do Letter No. 23011/11/2013(FRA), Government of India, Ministry of Tribal Affairs.

were granted in the name of VSSs.[138]

The Rules under the Forest Rights Act 2006, referred to the Gram Sabha as defined in PESA in its application to the Scheduled Areas. However the administrative 'village' under the AP Panchayat Raj Act 1994 at the Gram Panchayat level was adopted for the purpose of implementing the Forest Rights Act in Andhra Pradesh. This poses the problem of an unwieldy Gram Sabha which cannot function as required, particularly in passing any resolution on the claims with two-thirds quorum (amended to one-half in 2012) as required under the Forest Rights Act.[139]

2.9 Tribal Land Rights Movements

Protests over ST land rights are to be understood in the context of social, economic and political conditions during a specific period. Tribal revolts have generally been evoked by the struggle for survival. The revolts have largely been against the oppressive policies of both the government and the land proprietary class. As a consequence of these revolts, the state was drawn to bring systems in place for special protection of STs. There were altogether 70 major tribal revolts during the 200 years of British rule in India.[140]

There are three phases which can be identified in the tribal movements:

---

138. Rao, Trinadha P. A status paper prepared for the 'Public Hearing on Community Forest Rights', organised by CFR Learning and Advocacy group and Adivasi Janjati Adhikar Manch (AJAM) and other networks, at Constitution Club of India, New Delhi, 2013.
139. Reddy, M. Gopinath, K. Anil Kumar, P. Trinadha Rao and Oliver Springate-Baginski. Obstructed Access to Forest Justice: An Institutional Analysis of the Implementation of Rights Reform in Andhra's Forested Landscapes, Ippg: Manchester, 2010.
140. Raghavaiah, V. *Tribal Revolts, Andhra Pradesh,* Adimjati Sevak Sangha, Nellore, 1971.

(1) During the British period, most of the revolts were against the policies of the state affecting the traditional control of the tribals over their resources;
(2) Political struggles against the exploitation by the non-STs and appropriation of tribal land; and
(3) The opposition to the role of the state, particularly in the displacement of STs, and state-induced marginalisation after the advent of globalisation.

2.9.1 Tribal Struggles: Beginnings

The tribal revolts in Andhra Pradesh ensued on seven occasions. The first of the revolts led by Rambhoopati took place in 1802-1803. It is popularly known as the Rampa Fituri, or Rampa Rebellion, named after Rampa near Chodavaram in the East Godavari district of Andhra Pradesh. A second revolt around 1862 was directed against the *muttadars* (petty tribal *zamindars*), who supported the British. The third revolt around 1879 led by Chandraiah, Sambaiah, Thamman Dora and Ambul Reddy was also in the Rampa country. The fourth occasion on which a tribal uprising took place between 1922-1924 occurred under the leadership of Alluri Sri Rama Raju. While all these revolts had taken place in the coastal Andhra region, in the Telangana part of the Nizam's state, tribal revolts had taken place on two occasions. In 1842, Captain Blunt's Troops were attacked by Bastar Gonds forcing Captain Blunt to withdraw. Again, in 1941 a sporadic uprising of the Gonds and Kolam led by Komram Bheemu took place in the Adilabad District of the Telangana area in the erstwhile Nizam's state.[141]

Muttadars introduced new *abkari* (excise) regulations on account of which the local tribals were not allowed to tap toddy even for their domestic consumption. The imposition of several new taxes on the people led to a large number of

141. Raghavaiah, V. Unrest in Andhra Pradesh in A.R. Desai (ed.), *Peasant Struggles in India*, Oxford University Press: Bombay, 1979, p. 176.

litigations between the *zamindar*, tribals and the *muttadars*. In several cases, the *zamindars* obtained ex-party decrees and attached the property of the tribals. The police helped the *zamindars* and the confiscation of *muttas* and the oppression of the people resulted in uprisings against the *zamindari* authority in 1859, 1861 and 1862.

Few forms of taxation could have affected the peasants of Rampa more directly than taxes on toddy. From March to June, when the *podu* (shifting cultivation) fields were cleared and food stocks were low, the hill men would live on palmyra and sago palm toddy. Not surprisingly, they reacted by refusing to pay the new taxes which was the last straw—the spark that fired the train of growing discontent with the *mansabdar's* regime. Almost at once, on March 13, 1879, the Rampa rebellion began.[142]

The revolt of the people of Rampa was clearly against the State's encroachment over their traditional rights over forest resources and those who had profited from their exploitation. Restrictions on *podu*, creation of forest reserves, increased axe tax, introduction of opium into the hills for revenue as well as for the subjugation of tribals, prevention of the customary right to make toddy and collection of forest produce were the measures that drove the tribal people of Rampa to rebel repeatedly.[143]

Thus, one can see that peasant revolts occurred when their traditional socio-economic order is under attack, when capitalist classes are either emerging from within the society or intruding on it from the outside. One finds precisely the same process at work in the peasant revolts of late medieval Europe, and of colonial Burma and Vietnam in the early 20th

142. Sullivan to Chief Sec. 9 September (1879), Ibid; Joint Magistrate, Chodavaram, to District Magistrate, March 18, 1879, MJP, No, 313, March 25, 1879, In the Settlement of 1879-80, a small *chigurupannu* was incorporated in the *muttadar's 'kattubadi'*.
143. Arnold, David, op. cit.

century.[144]

The observations of Haimendorf are worth noting here:

> From our point of view, the history of the Rampa Rebellion is important in two respects. It shows, firstly, that aboriginals, even if inherently not of warlike character, are capable of considerable efforts when driven to extremities, and secondly, that it is both inexpedient and dangerous to allow the control and exploitation of aboriginal population to fall into the hands of unscrupulous outsiders, who although not directly responsible to the government, are backed by the authority of the police and the law courts.[145]

In 1832, the disturbances in the district and in Parlakhemundi *Zamindari* of Ganjam rose to such severity that the government was compelled to appoint Russell, a revenue board member, as Special Commissioner to suppress the revolt, arming him with extraordinary powers and a large military force.[146]

According to Haimendorf, while in reality this insurrection cannot be called a tribal struggle or a popular revolt like the Rampa rebellion, it was nevertheless successful. The prolonged defiance of law and order by tribals in the hilly areas of Vishakhapatnam and East Godavari agencies opened the eyes of the government to the gravity of the problem in the area. It realized that the tribal people living in these areas required special protection. The British authorities decided once again to give special measures to the Agency people for their development. It was felt that they

---

144. Hilton, op. cit., pp. 114-18; James C. Scott. *The Moral Economy of the Peasant Rebellion and Subsistence in Southeast Asia,* New Haven, 1976, exp. Ch. 4 in Rebellious Hillmen, 1839-1924 by David Arnold, in *Subaltern Studies-I*, Ranjita Guha (ed.), OUP, Delhi, 1986.
145. Haimendorf, Christopher von Furer. Aboriginal Rebellions in the Deccan, *Man in India,* Vol. 25, 1945 cited by P. Kamal Manohar Rao and D.L. Prasad Rao, *Tribal Movements in AP,* 1982, pp. 353-72.
146. Francis, W., op. cit., pp. 318-9.

required a more protective approach rather than a merely administrative one. This led to the allocation of subjects of tribal legislation and tribal welfare from the centre to the state.[147] The Andhra Pradesh Agency Rules 1924 was made to govern the Agency areas through the District Collector, designating her/him as an Agent to the Government.

An uprising of Gonds and Kolams in the Adilabad District of Hyderabad in 1940 occurred on account of the land and forest policy which ran directly counter to the needs and legitimate rights of the aboriginal people. By the late thirties, the tribals of Adilabad District were subjected to double oppression, one by the non-tribals who encroached upon their agricultural land and the other by the forest officials who expanded the boundaries of the reserved forest at the expense of their traditional habitat. The resultant conflict culminated in the death of ten Gonds in police firing in the 1940s.[148] The alienation of their land in the plains and the curtailment of their rights in the forests, were greatly resented by the tribals. The tyrannies and extractions of the subordinate government servants working in the forest and police departments further exasperated them.[149]

There are two main factors that can be traced to the tribal revolts that occurred in Andhra Pradesh and elsewhere in the country. There was a clash of economic interests between the tribals and non-tribals, and secondly, exploitation and oppression led to the tribal revolts. The other major factor was the clash of cultures of the tribals and the non-tribal vested interests which often led to social oppression by the non-tribals, ultimately leading to militant tribal movements.[150]

---

147. Raghavaiah, V. *Tribal Revolts*, Andhra Pradesh Adimjati Sevak Sangha, Nellore, 1971.
148. Reddy, Subba N. (1988), op. cit.
149. See Haimendorf, Christopher Von Furer (1945), op. cit., pp. 5-17.
150. Rao, Siva Rama Krishna C. and A. Bobbili. Tribal Movements in Andhra Pradesh: A Short History, in K. Murali Manohar, P. Ramaiah, and C. Sivaramakrishna Rao (eds.), *Political Economy of Tribal Development*, Indian Institute of Public Administration, Warangal. 1985.

2.9.2 Tribal Struggle in the Post-Independence Period

The non-ST hold over land continued unabated during the Nizam's Government in the State of Hyderabad. Paradoxically, this took a new shape in the period 1947-57 with the dawn of the Telangana peasant movement (1946-51). This movement helped to bring a Tenancy Legislation protecting the interests of the tenant's land rights. The genesis of the peasant struggle in Telangana can be traced to the Srikakulam movement of 1969 which was inspired by the Naxalbari movement in West Bengal.

The Naxalite movement in 1969 aimed to seize the State's power through an agrarian revolution. This movement is said to have succeeded in regaining control over 3 lakh acres of ST land in the five districts of Warangal, Karimnagar, Adilabad, West and East Godavari Districts in the State of Andhra Pradesh.[151] Land Transfer Regulations 1 of 70 was itself promulgated after the Naxalite movement in 1969.

Mass-based organisations affiliated to the left political parties with strong rural roots often took up the cause of tribals in land disputes in the post-1970s. Such organisations include the Raitu Coolie Sangham under CPI-ML New Democracy, which was earlier known as CPI-ML Prajapandha and involved in land issues in East Godavari; and the Agency Girijan Sangham, the frontal group of the revolutionary party CPI-ML, operating in both East and West Godavari. Andhra Pradesh Girijana Sangham, a splinter organisation of CPI-M, began focusing on tribal land issues in the post-1990s in the Agency areas of West Godavari District. These organisations have been mobilising the tribal communities for retrieval of their land from the possession of non-tribals through land occupation movements.

The collective action of the tribals under the leadership of the Andhra Pradesh Communist Committee of Revolutionary (APCCR) created a scare among the non-ST

---

151. *A Report on Godavari Valley*, Girijana Ryotanga Porata Charita, CPI (ML), 1977.

cultivators who had settled in the tribal areas. They could not approach the courts as they had illegally acquired ST land. They began putting pressure on the state government to use police force to curb the collective action of STs on the plea that they were being led by the APCCR (Naxalite) cadres. This resulted in the state government establishing police camps throughout the Agency Areas of East and West Godavari, Khammam and Warangal districts. A police camp was also set up in Kondamodalu.[152]

The tribal movement of Kondamodulu village consisting of twelve hamlets in Devipatnam Mandal of East-Godavari district focused on the land struggle against landlords who used to control tribal land illegally. Shivaiah Patrudu, a non-ST landlord, along with his other kinfolk, used to dictate terms in the Agency area. The feudal lord's rule over the area was challenged by the 'Girijana Sangham' which was founded in 1967 by the STs of the area, and is an outfit of the CPI (ML). The movement began in 1968 and gained momentum between July 1981 and November 1982 when the STs occupied the land controlled by the landlord and sowed paddy. Having taken control over 3,000 acres of land in that area, the movement spread to other areas as the neighbouring *mandals* of West Godavari District.

Post-1986, tribal areas of Devipatnam Mandal in East Godavari district witnessed land occupation movement by STs with the support of Andhra Pradesh Ryutu Coolie Sangham, a frontal group of CPI (ML) New Democracy. STs questioned the fraudulently obtained settlement *pattas* by non-STs over their land during the survey and settlement period of 1970-76. The STs occupied such land and restrained non-ST settlement *patta* holders from entering a stretch of nearly 2,000 acres land. [153]

In 1996, the STs in the area strongly put forward their claim that the entire land in Scheduled Areas belonged to

152. Rao, Jayaprakash P., op. cit.
153. Rao, Trinadha P. (2007), op. cit.

them, while the non-STs continued to show the title deeds of the land they held. This led to a controversy regarding the contradictory facts presented in the 1902 and the 1933 Resettlement Survey Register (RSR). Such controversies often took a violent turn during the struggle. Violent attacks on the non-STs resulted in retaliation wherein both sections recorded loss of life. A civil war like situation resulted from this hostility. The incidents at Manugopala and Busarajupalli are illustrative of this. A group of non-STs raided the tribal hamlet over a land issue in Manugopala village on March 21, 1996. On August 5, 1997, during a confrontation at Busarajupalli, the STs scared the non-STs by shooting arrows and thrashing a few men.[154]

A few non-governmental organisations such as Laya and Sakthi, based in the tribal area of East Godavari District, have raised the tribal land question in coastal areas and parts of Telangana region in Andhra Pradesh through various tribal initiatives, without confining themselves to court litigation. Armed with the required knowledge and skills to understand the land records, a section of the STs triggered a land movement which resulted in the state level officials agreeing to convene a meeting to settle all outstanding issues during the year 1997. Further, the land issues of Godavari District came under the consideration of Andhra Pradesh High Court on several occasions. One such case was Payam Gangamma and Vasudha Mishra and Others (WP CC No 1381/97). The High Court passed a landmark judgement agreeing with the concern of STs and issued directions to be followed during the survey of lands to know the actual land possessors. The High Court directed the revenue authorities to conduct land survey in the presence of tribal stakeholders after furnishing the relevant land documents and maps. These changes have

---

154. Kumar, Arun. From Landlessness to Ownership: The Tribal Struggle for Property Rights in Govinda Chandra Rath (ed.), *Tribal Development in India*, Sage Publications, New Delhi, 2006.

brought confidence in the tribal youth in resolving the land conflicts on their own.[155]

Even during the talks in 2004 with the government on the issue of land, the People's War Group (Maoists) and CPI-ML (Janasakthi) put forth several demands, as the lowering of the ceiling limits on land, and distribution of surplus land, including the endowment and other land at the disposal of the government, to the poorer sections. The talks with the government pushed the state to constitute the Koneru Rangarao Land Committee to look into the land issues and study the land laws for recommendations to improve the agrarian situation. The Committee came up with several recommendations to protect the interest of tribal land by effective implementation of ST protective land transfer regulations and cancellation of settlement *pattas* obtained by non-STs fraudulently. However, no amendments were made to plug the loopholes in the law. On the other hand, the circulars issued by the government for implementation are also not enforced.

Thus, the on and off movements for political contestation by the non-governmental organisations and political parties for increasing access to land justice for STs created only a partial impact in enforcement of ST protective land laws.

155. Trinadha Rao, P. (2007), op. cit.

3

Conclusion

The extent of land alienation in the Scheduled Areas is a cause for public concern. The process of land alienation has not stopped even after the promulgation of ST protective land laws due to weak enforcement of the laws. STs have lost their land due to multiple attacks, including the exploitative mechanism compounded by forcible acts of the non-ST settlers and the interventions of the state in dispossessing their land. The Forest Department interventions are another source of resource displacement of STs. The ST land alienation issue is further complicated by the mainstream political parties due to their tilt towards the non-ST vote bank policies. The special protection extended for ST rights through various legislations with the support of main opposition parties are part of the welfare measures of the State, but without the political will to actually convert them into a reality. As a result of land alienation, the ST have lost livelihood and their cultural linkage with the natural resources. Perhaps, the tribal belt will experience more and more incursions of the non-ST and industrial interests in future and lose its character despite the Fifth Schedule of the Constitution. The magnitude of the problem is of national importance and needs to be tackled and solved through Parliamentary intervention and effective enforcement of the laws.

Denial of the land rights of STs is essentially due to the

introduction of an alien land administration which marginalized ST. At the root of the problem lies the fact that the state policy tends to be biased against STs and which in turn perpetuates land alienation.

Large chunks of land were transferred from the non-ST proprietors of *mukasas, zamindars* and non-ST claimant *muttadars*. There are no measures to check the influx of non-ST because the non-ST land tenure administrators' declared an open policy to hand over the land to either ST or non-ST on lease by grant of conditional *pattas* called *'krishika patta'* in *mukasa* villages and *'veesa badi patta'* in estate villages to raise the land revenue. The British land survey policy was intended to generate revenue by land survey to determine land holders, unmindful of tribal interests. Land alienation in favour of non-ST started during the survey periods of 1902 onwards. STs, who have no idea of legitimacy of the survey records and determination of boundaries except earmarking traditional boundaries of hills and trees, lost control over the resources. The internal migration among the tribal communities further weakened the levels of their articulation in land alienation matters. The original tribal inhabitants moved to other places and the new tribal entrants of the village are not in a position to question the occupations of the non-ST in the villages.

The laissez-faire policy of the state also worked against the interests of STs. The initial Act framed in 1917 restricted the transfer of land between STs and non-STs without obtaining consent from the Agent or the prescribed officer. But there is no special machinery set up to check the illegal transfers or making a special provision applying to non-ST proprietors of land tenures like *mutta*, estate, *mahals*, etc. The law was made; but no specific provision was made to protect the interests of STs by imposing restrictions on land registrations in favour of non-STs during the surveys carried out in 1902 and 1932 in government (*ryotwari*) villages. This is a major lacuna in the land policy governing ST land alienation issues. Even in the Land Transfer Regulations made in 1959 no rules were made till 1969 for its operationalisation. There was no change in the evidence law to give credence to the oral evidence of STs whose value system was based on verbal rather on written form in administrative or court enquiries. Similarly, the Land Transfer Regulations 1 of 70 was restricted to prospective land transfers between non-STs without covering the past land transactions. This gives a lot of scope to non-STs to retain the land in their hold, and litigation never ends. The legal presumption clause under the Land Transfer Regulations 1 of 70, which advocates that the land situated in the Scheduled Areas once belonged to tribals unless the contrary is proved, remained a presumptive statement, rather than a useful legal provision in the context of the legal framework. As a result, the law has acted as a mediating agency in a significant manner in favour of the non-STs in change of land ownership and use.

The open policy of the state to invite non-STs to tribal areas by offering land negated the rights of STs. This is contrary to a tribal society's definition of land ownership and relationship. Institutional and legal frameworks are the products dictated by the dominant political and economic class through the government and public administration, which negated the customary right of STs over land. Further, the institutional framework gives more credence to the written records rather than to oral testimony and traditional land tenure systems. In fact, no provision under law was made to record or cover concealed land transactions held between STs and non-STs.

The STs have experienced displacement and loss of land and natural resources on which their cultural identities depend. They have also experienced the fundamental dynamics of power and inequality, in accessing land justice. The most fundamental inequality in the Scheduled Area is between the non-STs elites who are able to access administrative and legal structures of the state and the vast majority of STs who cannot do so.

The class division of STs and non-STs is best capitalized to consolidate vote banks by the political parties by promising the implementation of ST protective Land Transfer Regulations on one hand and diluting the same through other interventions in support of land occupation of non-STs in the Agency Tracts. Creating Scheduled Tribes Protection Cell in the framework of political parties and facilitating the tribal individuals to head the same, is a strategic intervention of the parties to capture the tribal vote banks. It is important to note, however, that the success of individuals in gaining access to the administrative or political or constitutional advisory bodies does not benefit STs at large. On the contrary, it runs counter to the interests of STs. The record of the TAC meetings also proves their nominal role in protecting the interest of STs.

The political parties take sides to favour the non-ST population in Agency Areas. This is evident from the proceedings of the TAC and the attempts made in 1988 to repeal the Land Transfer Regulations 1 of 70 to lure the non-ST voters. However, these attempts were negated by the STs and their supportive groups. Similarly in 1999, the non-STs were facilitated to construct houses in the Scheduled Areas by issuing possession certificates.

In 1969-1970, in an attempt to negate the Land Transfer Regulations 1 of 70 the Survey and Settlement Regulations 1 of 69, 2 of 69 and 2 of 70 were introduced after abolition of intermediary land tenure proprietorship. As described by Gunnar Myrdal in the famous *Asian Drama*[156], the role of the state in the case of the land alienation was that of a 'soft state' dominated by powerful non-ST interests that exploit the power of the State or administrative mechanisms to serve their own interests, rather than the interests of STs. Policies decided are often not enforced, if they are enacted at all.

In fact, the abolition of intermediary proprietors of land tenures is proclaimed to end the feudal mode of control over

---

156. Myrdal, Gunnar. *Asian Drama*, 1969, pp. 66, 277.

the resources. However, the state intervention further reproduced a legitimate non-ST land holding class in tribal areas. The provision of settlement of land to the non-ST *ryots*, if they have been in their occupation for a period of 8 years prior to the notified date under various Settlement Regulations is a 'proactive' provision. Even the ineligible non-ST encroachers secured regularization of land occupation under these Settlement Regulations, which are otherwise illegal under the Land Transfer Regulations 1 of 70. No enquiry was made under these Land Transfer Regulations purposefully by the Settlement Officers before granting *pattas* in favour of non-STs. Moreover, in matters of land settlement, even the legal process provides ample scope for manipulation and corruption. Land alienation in many cases have turned STs into bonded labourers or underpaid agrarian labourers on their own land.

Bringing the Scheduled Tracts into Fifth Schedule under the Constitution is also based on the 'segregated isolationistic' approach which had its roots in the Government of India Act 1870, which intended to specify tracts as 'Scheduled Tracts'. A diametrically opposite approach sanctified by the Planning Commission of India is the 'policy of assimilation' of STs into the mainstream of national life. This policy change helps to maintain the landed interest of the non-STs in the Scheduled Areas. Because of this policy, a strong non-ST class has emerged in the Scheduled Areas. The non-ST entrepreneurship in the Scheduled Areas is considered to be a vehicle for tribal development. Instead, the STs are pushed to the margins. The dominant non-ST elite class controls the political and administrative structures and sustains their interests in tribal areas.

The fact is also that the Land Transfer Regulations 1 of 70 is an outcome of the Srikakulam Naxalite Movement. The agenda of land reforms in Koneru Land Committee was put forward by Maoists before the government of Andhra Pradesh in 2005. However, the left parties is conspicuously absent in following up on implementation of protective Land

Transfer Regulations. The State is unwilling to implement the Government Orders issued basing on the recommendations of Koneru Land Committee. No single circular is in actual implementation.This helps the non-ST to show their legitimacy over the land in their hold secured through legal interventions.

The Land Transfer Regulations prohibits transfer of all immovable property in Scheduled Areas of the state unless the recipient is a ST or a cooperative society whose members are all ST. Even a transfer from a non-ST to another non-ST is prohibited. The presumption is that any immovable property in the possession of a non-ST in the Scheduled Area has been obtained by transfer from an ST. It is for the non-ST to prove their legal ownership of the land; if he fails to do so, the land is to be taken over by the government and distributed to eligible STs.

The Fifth Schedule speaks of the power to regulate or prohibit or restrict the transfer of land and the allotment of land in the Scheduled Areas. The Supreme Court in Samata vs. State of Andhra Pradesh (AIR 1997 SC 3297) held that the provisions of the Fifth Schedule and those of the Land Transfer Regulations must be read together.

The weak enforcement machinery, non transparency and lack of accountability in the administration of land justice through Special Courts are in effect a collusion with the powerful sections of the non-STs. The Special Deputy Tahsildars who file cases on behalf of STs under the Land Transfer Regulations against the illegal non-ST occupants of land, never file appeals if they did not succeed in the lower court level. The State machinery is unwilling to evict non-STs by pursuing further legal recourse at the higher judicial level. Even where orders in favour of STs are issued, the authorities more often do not carry them out. These result in a total lack of faith in the administrative and judicial system to administer law and order or justice. The Supreme Court had characterized the competition between STs and non-STs in accessing land justice in the context of Land Transfer

Regulations 1 of 70 as 'a race between a handicapped one-legged person and an able bodied two legged person'[157].

Thus, the failure of the government and political parties to uphold the law and Constitution in this regard leaves the STs with no other option but to seek other political means to ensure justice. One such option is the direct repossession of alienated lands with the support of frontal groups of the CPI (ML) groups.

Tribal land rights protection requires a rethinking on the part of the government about governance structures to bring about an equitable balance of rights and responsibilities between non-STs and the tribal community as well as the state, in usage of land and their relationship with land. The inclusiveness of STs in the decision-making process in land disputes should be an essential element to inspire confidence in the administration of justice in land matters. These land conflicts can run along different and less predictable lines and can range from local to regional or state level, involving a wide diversity of government institutions and identities.

3.1 Recommendations

3.1.1 Legislative Changes

1. Retrospective effect is to be given to all Land Transfer Laws from 1917 onwards in Andhra Area and from 1949 (1359 Fasli) onwards in Telangana Area.
2. Enforcement officers must be empowered to exercise suo moto powers under Land Transfer Regulations (LTR) in filing LTR cases without any period of limitation or constraints in the name of reasonable period. This legal change is required to avoid the often used res judicata principle in court cases.
3. There must be a special provision to record concealed land transactions held between STs and non-STs as well as among the non-STs in land records.

---

157. P. Rami Reddy & Others vs. State of AP & Another. (1988) 22 Reports (SC) 364.

4. The penal provision for violation of Land Transfer Regulations should be extended to the officers who disregard the orders issued by Courts or Government in implementation of Land Transfer Regulations.
5. The oral evidence of STs in land cases should be given an overriding importance over any contrary documentary evidence produced by non-ST parties.
6. To ensure the resumption of alienated land, a tribunal with members of ST community representatives, tribal rights activists and government officials should be set up at the Integrated Tribal Development Agency level and at the lower level Gram Sabha should be given power to adjudicate land disputes. The decision at the Integrated Tribal Development Agency level should be made final and the interference of the High Court should be permitted only in the case of clear violations and without staying operation of the orders passed by the Tribunal.
7. The provisions enabling filing of appeals against the orders passed by the authorities, under both the Land Transfer Regulations and the Ryotwari Settlement Regulations should be amended to enable the tribal parties to question the irregularity or illegality of the orders given in favour of the non-STs earlier.
8. The jurisdiction of civil courts in entertaining the civil suits through injunction or declaration title over the land situated in the Scheduled Areas at the instance of the non-STs should be barred.

3.1.2 Land Administration for Effective Implementation of Land Transfer Regulations

1. Separate machinery should be set up for restoration of alienated ST land and filing of appeals against in favourable orders.
2. Updating land records by physical verification and incorporating the names of actual cultivators in the revenue records is necessary. These records, in addition

to the court orders, must be accessible to STs at the Gram Panchayat level.

3. The government land must be made accessible to STs and illegal non-ST encroachers should be evicted.
4. At the State level, a committee must be set up with the representatives of the government, civil society organisations and experts on tribal land issues to monitor the implementation of Land Transfer Regulations and give timely directions from time to time to the enforcing authorities.
5. Similar committees must be set up at the level of Integrated Tribal Development Agency.
6. The Special Deputy Collectors in the Scheduled Areas must be given postings after a compulsory intensive training on Land Transfer Regulations and other relevant laws. Frequent sensitization programmes on ST land rights need to be organised for both Special Deputy Collectors and other enforcement machinery.
7. The Integrated Tribal Development Agencies must be empowered to control the influx or infiltration of the non-ST population by taking steps in the light of Land Transfer Regulation provisions, and in coordination of all licensing departments, should be assigned to check the establishment of shops, enterprises and constructions for housing or for any other commercial purpose.
8. Police interference on behalf of the non-STs and against the interest of STs should be restrained and erring officials should be punished.

References

1. *Andhra Pradesh District Gazetteers,* East Godavari district, Government of Andhra Pradesh, Central Press, Hyderabad, 1976.
2. Andhra Pradesh Girijan Welfare Students and Youth Union vs. State of AP W.P.No 1755/90 dated December 5, 1984.
3. Adarsha Adivasi Mahila Samithi & Others vs. Agent to the Government Khammam & Others. 2003 (5) ALD 284.
4. *All India Reporter (AIR),* Supreme Court (SC) p. 389-404, AIR Publication, Nagpur, March 1985.
5. Amrendra Prapat Singh, Appellant vs. Tej Bahadur Prajapati and Others, AIR 2004 Supreme Court, p. 3782.
6. Arnold David. Agent. Godavari, to Chief Secretary. July 29, 1884, G.O. 2618, Jdl. September 27, 1909, Godavari Statistical Appendix, pp. 413-14 cited in Rebellious Hillmen: The Gudem-Rampa Risings 1839-1924 in *Subaltern Studies-I: Writings on South Asian History and Society*, Ranjita Guha (ed.), Oxford University Press, Delhi, 1986.
7. Arnold David. Committee of Circuit's Report, 1787, p. 4 cited in Rebellious Hillmen in *Subaltern Studies-I*, Ranjit Guha (ed.), Oxford University Press, Delhi, 1986.
8. Ashok vs. Baba Rao and Another. 2002 (6) ALT 296.
9. Ashokvardhan, C. *Tribal Land Rights in India.* Centre for Rural Studies, LBS National Academy of Administration, Mussoorie, 2006.
10. Balagopal, K. Pitting the Tribals Against the Non-tribal Poor, *Economic and Political Weekly*, May 27, 1989, p. 1151.
11. Balagopal, K. Foreword to book by P.Trinadha Rao, *Land Rights of Adivasis*, Laya Publications, Visakhapatnam, 2004.

12. Balagopal, K. Land Unrest in Andhra Pradesh III: Illegal Acquisition in Tribal Areas, *Economic and Political Weekly*, October 6, 2007, p. 4031.
13. Banerjee, Abhijit and Lakshmi Iyer. *Colonial Land Tenure, Electoral Competition and Public Goods in India,* A Working Paper, 2008. See www.hbs.edu/research/pdf/08-062).
14. Baviskar, A. The Fate of the Forest: Conservation and Tribals Rights, *Economic and Political Weekly*, September 17, 1994.
15. Baviskar, A. *The Politics of Being* "Indigenous" in Bengt G. Karlsson and Tanka B. Subba (eds.), *Indigeneity in India,* Kegan Paul, London in De La Cadena and Starn, 2007:8.
16. Bengwayan, Michael A. *Intellectual and Cultural Property Rights of Indigenous and Tribal Peoples in Asia,* Report of Minority Rights Group International, 379, Brixton Road, London, SW9 7DE (UK), 2003.
17. Beteille, Andre. *Studies in Agrarian Social Structure,* Oxford University Press, Oxford, 1974.
18. Bhowmik, K.L. *Tribal India: A Profile in Indian Ethnology* cited in Supreme Court case (3 SCC 429; 2004 SCC CRI 818), 2004.
19. Bhushan, Bharath M. *Land Rights of Women in Andhra Pradesh – A Status Paper* (Mimeo), Rural Development Institute, Hyderabad, 2011.
20. Bijoy, C.R. Adivasi Rights and Struggles of Autonomy: A Review of the Indian Experience, in K. Krishnan (ed.), *Adivasi Groups,* (Mimeo), 2000.
21. Bijoy, C.R. and K. Ravi Raman. Muthunga, The Real Story: Adivasi Movements to Recover Land, *Economic and Political Weekly*, Vol. 38, No. 20, May 17, 2003.
22. Brennan, F. Parliamentary Responses to the Mabo Decision, in M.A. Stephenson (ed.), *Mabo, The Native Title Legislation: A Legislative Response to the High Court Decision*, Queensland University Press, St Lucia, 1995, pp. 1–25.
23. Brockett, C.D. *Land, Power and Poverty: Agrarian Transformation and Political Conflict in Central America,* Unwin Hyman, 1990, pp. 23-26.
24. Burman, B.K. Transfer and Alienation of Tribal Land, in *Tribal Development in India,* Inter-India Publications, New Delhi, 1982, p. 77.
25. CESS, *Report on Human Development*, Begampet, Hyderabad, 2007.

26. Ch. Satyanarayana vs. The Agent to Government & District Collector, Visakapatnam-WP 6065/1979,High Court of Andhra Pradesh, Hyderabad.
27. Colletti, Lucio. *Early Writings-Karl Marx*, Penguin Books, London, 1975, p. 20.
28. Deogaonkar, S.G. *Tribal Administration and Development*, Concept Publishing Company, New Delhi, 1994.
29. Deputy Collector vs. Venkata Ramanaiah & Another-AIR, 1996 S.C, p. 224.
30. Desai, M., S.M. Rudolph and Ashok Rudra (eds.). *Agrarian Power and Agricultural Productivity in South Asia*, Oxford University Press, Delhi, 1984.
31. Deva, Satya. Alienation and Administration in Developing Countries, *Mainstream*, July 1981, pp. 126-7 quoted in Ramdas Rupavath, *Tribal Land Alienation and Political Movements: Socio-Economic Patterns of South India*, Cambridge Scholars Publications, UK, 2009.
32. Dhanagare, D.M. Subaltern Consciousness and Populism—Two Approaches in the Study of Social Movements in India, *Social Scientist*, 16, No. 11, November 1988, p. 20.
33. D'Souza, Nafisa Goga. Landholding Systems in Tribal Areas, *Social Action*, Vol. 41, No. 1, ISI, New Delhi, January-March 1991, pp. 345-50.
34. Ellickson, R. Property in Land, 103(6), *Yale Law Journal*, 1993, pp. 1344-1362.
35. Elwin, Verrier. *New Deal for Tribal India*, Ministry of Home Affairs, New Delhi, 1963, p. 49.
36. Fernandes, Walter. Land Reforms, Ownership Pattern and Alienation of Tribal Livelihood, *Social Action*, Vol. 46, October-December 1996, p. 428.
37. Francis, W. *Madras District Gazetteers*, Vizagapatnam, printed by the Superintendent, Government Press, (Mimeo) copy, Vol. I, 1907, pp. 310-11.
38. Gadde Nagabhushanamma vs Government of AP, 1999(5) ALD 430, Hyderabad.
39. Gangamma P. vs. Vasudha Misra (District Collector, West Godavari-1998(2) ALD 35, Hyderabad.
40. Ghurye, G.S. *The Scheduled Tribes* (Third Edition), Popular Prakashan, Bombay, 1963.
41. *Godavari District Gazetteer*, Government Press, Madras, 1907, p. 101.

42. Government of India. *Report of the Scheduled Areas of Scheduled Tribes Commission (1960-61)*, Government of India Press, New Delhi, Vol. I, p. 1.
43. Haimendorf, C. von Furer. *Tribes of India: The Struggle for Survival*, Oxford University Press, New Delhi, 1985.
44. Haimendorf, C. von Furer. Cited from pp. 203-8; F.R. Hemingway, *Madras District Gazetteers: Godavari* (Madras, 1915), p. 67; Thurston, *Castes and Tribes*, III, p. 355. IV, pp. 64-5; Cain, Bhadrachelam and Rekapalli Taluqas, p. 33.
45. Haimendorf, C. von Furer. Aboriginal Rebellions in the Deccan, *Man in India*, Vol. 25, 1945 cited by P. Kamal Manohar Rao and D.L. Prasad Rao, *Tribal Movements in Andhra Pradesh*, 1982, pp. 353-72.
46. Heredia, Rudolf C. Tribal History, Living Word or Dead Letter, *Economic and Political Weekly*, April 29, 2000.
47. Hilton, op. cit., pp. 114-18; James C. Scott. (1986) *The Moral Economy of the Peasant Rebellion and Subsistence in Southeast Asia*, (New Haven, 1976), exp. Ch. 4 in Rebellious Hillmen, 1839-1924 by David Arnold, in *Subaltern Studies-I*, Ranjita Guha (ed.), OUP, Delhi.
48. Hooja, Meenakshi. *Policies and Strategies for Tribal Development: Focus on the Central Tribal Belt*, Rawat Publications, Jaipur, 2004, pp. 19-20.
49. International Labour Organization. *Indigenous and Tribal Peoples*, Geneva, 1994.
50. Istvan, Meszaros. *Marx's Theory of Alienation*, Aakar Books, New Delhi, 2006.
51. Jagannath, Ambagudia. Tribal Rights, Dispossession and the State in Orissa, *Economic and Political Weekly*, August 14, 2010, Vol. xiv, No. 33.
52. Jha, J.C. The Changing Land System of the Tribals of Chota Nagpur, 1771-1831, 1989; *Changing Land Systems and Tribals in Eastern India in the Modern Period*, Tarasankar Banerjee (ed.), Subarnarekha, Calcutta, pp. 80-90.
53. K. Mahalaxmi & Another vs. Government of Andhra Pradesh & Others, 2000 (5) ALD 588.
54. Kakarla Nageswara Rao and Other vs Government of AP rep by its Secretary (Tribal Welfare), Department Hyderabad, 1995(3)ALT 164.
55. Kandula Brahmaiah vs. The Deputy Collector (Tribal Welfare)

Rampachodavaram, E.G. Dist. W.P. 2169/1981 Dated December 10, 1986-unreported.

56. Karuppaiyan, E. Alienation of Tribal Land in Tamil Nadu, *Economic and Political Weekly*, September 9, 2000, pp. 3343-34; see also Nandita Singh, Emerging Problems of Ownership and Exploitation of Communal Land in Tribal Society in *Man in India*, Vol. 77, 1997, pp. 233-34; Gupta, Smita, Tribal Land Alienation in Kanke Anchal, *The Administrator*, Vol. 36, No. 2, 1991, p. 873.
57. Kola Mahalaxmi vs. Agent to Government, Khammam & Others. 1999(6) ALD 718).
58. Koppula Suramma vs. Government of AP Social Welfare Department & others, 2001(3)ALT 501.
59. Kulkarni, Sharad. Maharashtra: Adivasi, Law and Social Justice, *Economic and Political Weekly*, Vol. xx (28), 1985, pp. 1171-4.
60. Kumar, S. Adivasis of South Orissa: Enduring Poverty, *Economic and Political Weekly*, Vol. 36, No. 43, October 27-November 2, 2001; Dietrich, G. Dams and People: Adivasi Land Rights, *Economic and Political Weekly*, Vol. 35 No. 38, September 16-22, 2000; and Virginius Xaxa. Tribes as Indigenous People of India, *Economic and Political Weekly*, Vol. XXIV, No. 51, December 18, 1999, pp. 3589-95.
61. M. Suresh Bhargava & Another vs. State of AP & Others. 1989 (2) ALT 516.
62. Maheshwari, Uma R. Polavaram Rehabilitation via Forced Consensus, *Economic and Political Weekly*, June 23, 2007.
63. Mahipal. Panchayats in Fifth Scheduled Areas, *Economic and Political Weekly*, May 6, 2000.
64. Malayappan, R.S. Report of the Special Development Officer, Government of AP. Hyderabad, 1984, p. 8.
65. Manohar, Murali K. and B. Janardhan Rao. Land Alienation in Tribal Areas in K. Murali Manohar, P. Ramaiah and C. Sivakrishna Rao (eds.), *Political Economy of Tribal India*, IIPA, Warangal, 1985, pp. 63-94.
66. Manohar, Murali K. Political Economy of Tribal Development: A Theme Paper, in *Political Economy of Tribal Development*, K. Murali Manohar, P. Ramaiah, and C. Sivaramakrishna Rao (eds.), Indian Institute of Public Administration, Warangal, 1985.

67. Manohar, Murali K. and Janardhan B. Rao. Tribal Agricultural Labour: An Enquiry into the Depeasantization Process in Buddhadev Chaudhari (Ed.) *Tribal Transformation in India*, Vol. I, Inter-India Publications, New Delhi, 1992.
68. Minutes of the APTAC meeting held on December 23, 1988, Hyderabad.
69. Matlhy, T.J. *Ganjam Manual*, Madras, 1918, p. 139.
70. Ministry of Rural Development, Department of Land Resources Report, GoI, 2000.
71. Ministry of Rural Development, Government of AP, *D.V.L.N. Murthy Committee: Report on Tribal Land Issues*, Hyderabad, 2005.
72. Ministry of Rural Development, Government of AP. *J.M. Girglani Commission: Report on Tribal Land Issues*, Hyderabad, 2005.
73. Ministry of Rural Development, Government of AP. *Koneru Land Committee Report*, Hyderabad, 2006, p. 57.
74. Ministry of Social Welfare, Government of India. *Report of the Study Team on Social Welfare and Welfare of Backward Classes*, Vol. 1, 1959.
75. Ministry of Social Welfare Department, Government of India. *National Commission on Backward Areas Development Report*, June 1981, p. 50,
76. Ministry of Social Welfare, Government of Andhra Pradesh. *Note on Land Problems in Agency Areas of West Godavari*, Hyderabad, 1997.
77. Ministry of Tribal Affairs, Government of AP. *Report of the Task Force on Development of Tribal Areas* (Prof. Vidyarthi Committee), April 5, 1972.
78. Ministry of Tribal Welfare Department, Government of AP. *Land Reforms and Land Transfers Report*, Hyderabad, 1995.
79. Ministry of Tribal Affairs, Government of India. *Report of the Excluded and Partially Excluded Areas Sub-committee*, (Thakkar Committee), August 18, 1947.
80. Ministry of Tribal Affairs, Government of India, *Report of Commission for SC and ST*, Fifth Report, 1982-83, p. 28,
81. Ministry of Tribal Affairs, Government of India. *Draft National Policy on Tribals*, 2004.
82. Ministry of Tribal Affairs, Government of India. *D. Swaminadhan Tribal Policy Draft*, 2004.

83. Minutes of the APTAC meeting held on February 5, 1977, Hyderabad.
84. Minutes of APTAC meeting, Review of Action Taken (1979-80), Hyderabad.
85. Minutes of the APTAC meeting held on April 30, 1982, Hyderabad
86. Minutes of the APTAC meeting held on November 28, 1986, Hyderabad.
87. Minutes of the APTAC meeting held on February 14, 1994, Hyderabad.
88. Minutes of the APTAC meeting held on February 14, 1994, Hyderabad.
89. Minutes of the APTAC meeting held on November 17, 1995, Hyderabad.
90. Minutes of the APTAC meeting held on June 26, 1999, Hyderabad.
91. Minutes of the APTAC meeting held on April 12, 2000, Hyderabad.
92. Minutes of the APTAC meeting held on May 24, 2000, Hyderabad.
93. Minutes of APTAC meeting held on March 18, 2010, Hyderabad.
94. Mohan Lal, Morley. *Poverty Alleviation: The Indian Experience*, Himalaya Publishing House, Delhi, 1988, p. 386.
95. Mohanty, P.K. Development of Scheduled Castes and Scheduled Tribes in Independent India: Leads and Lags, *Journal of Rural Development*, Vol. 19(4), 2000, p. 551.
96. Mohapatro, Prafullo Chandro. *Dynamics of Tribal and Non-Tribal Interaction* in *Economic Development of Tribal India*, Ashish Publishing House, New Delhi, 1987.
97. Murthy, Linga. N. and Shiva Rama Krishna Rao C. Debt-Bondage in Tribal Areas—An Empirical Observation in book titled *Political Economy of Tribal Development*, K. Murali Manohar, P. Ramaiah and C. Sivarama Krishna Rao (eds.), Indian Institute of Public Administration, Warangal, 1985.
98. N. Durga Rao & Another vs. Special Deputy Collector (TW) Kota Ramachandrapuram W.G. Dist. & Others. 2003(6) ALD (NOC) 68.
99. Nath, N., D.K. Behera, Sarkar, R.M. (eds.). *The So-called Development, Displacement and Dispossession: An Analysis on Land and Forest Rights of the Project Affected People. Land and*

Forest Rights of the Tribals Today, Serials Publications, Delhi, 2006.
100. Nathan, D.G. Kekar and P. Walter (Eds.). *Civilizational Change: Markets and Privatization Among Indigenous Peoples. Globalization and Indigenous Peoples* in *Asia: Changing the Local-Global Interface*, Delhi: Sage Publications, 2004.
101. Omvedt, Gail. Capitalism and Globalization, Dalits and Adivasis, *Economic and Political Weekly*, November 19, 2005.
102. P. Gangamma vs. Vasudha Misra & Another. 1998(2) ALD 35.
103. P. Rami Reddy & Others vs. State of AP & Another. (1988) 22 Reports (SC) 364.
104. *Parliament Digest–Budget Session*, NCAS Publications, Pune, 2004, p. 53.
105. Parthasarathy et.al. *Peasant Movements and Changing Agrarian Structure in AP*, Department of Cooperation and Applied Economics, Andhra University, Visakhapatnam (Mimeo), 1979.
106. Patnaik, S.C. and S. Patel. *Impact of Modernization on Tribals: Economic Dualism and Path of Change (A Case Study of Malkangiri Sub-division in Koraput district)*, paper presented at the Seminar on 'Prospectus of Economic Development of Tribals of Koraput District' held in October (Mimeo), 1982, pp. 2-14.
107. Peters, P. The Erosion of Commons and the Emergence of Property: Problems for Social Analysis, in Hunt, R.C. and A. Gilman (eds.), *Property in Economic Context*, University Press of America, 1998, pp. 356-61.
108. Pinto, Ambrose. Fillip to Land Transfers Land Acquisition Bill, *Economic and Political Weekly*, December 5, 1988.
109. Planning Commission Report of the Steering Committee on the Empowering the Scheduled Tribes, Government of India, New Delhi, 2001, p. 91.
110. Planning Commission Report, Government of India, New Delhi, 2006.
111. Planning Commission Report of the Expert Group on *Development Issues to Deal with the Causes of Discontent, Unrest and Extremism*, GoI, India, 2008.
112. Radhakrishna, R. and Shovan Ray. *Handbook of Poverty in India: Perspectives, Policies, and Programmes*, Oxford University Press, New Delhi, 2006.
113. Raghavaiah, V. *Tribal Revolts, Andhra Pradesh*, Adimjati Sevak Sangha, Nellore, 1971.

114. Raghavaiah. V. Unrest in Andhra Pradesh in A.R. Desai (ed.) *Peasant Struggles in India*, Oxford University Press, Bombay, 1979, p. 176.
115. Ramanathan, U. Public Purpose: Points for Discussion, in W. Fernandes (ed.), *The Land Acquisition (Amendment) Bill 1998*, Indian Social Institute, New Delhi, 1999, pp. 19–24.
116. Ramanathan, U. Common Land and Common Property Resources in Land Reforms in India, in Praveen K. Jha (ed.), *Issues of Enquiry in Rural Madhya Pradesh*, Sage Publications, New Delhi, Vol. 7, 2002, p. 204.
117. Ramnath, Madhu. Surviving the Forest Rights Act: Between Scylla and Charybdis, *Economic and Political Weekly*, March 1, 2008.
118. Rao, B. Janardhana. *Land Alienation in Tribal Areas of Andhra Pradesh*, Kakatiya University, Warangal, 1987.
119. Rao, B. Janardhana. *Adivasis in India–Characterization of Transition and Development*, Adhyayana Publications, Warangal, 2000.
120. Rao, Jayaprakash P. The Struggle for Land: Tribal Revolts in Two Villages, in *Political Economy of Tribal Development*, K. Murali Manohar, P. Ramaiah and C. Sivaramakrishna Rao (eds.), Indian Institute of Public Administration, Warangal, 1985.
121. Rao, M.S.A. Non-tribal Colonization and Tribal Deprivation in Andhra, *Social Action*, ISI, New Delhi, Vol. 33, July-September 1983.
122. Rao, Sivaramakrishna C., and Bobbili, A. Tribal Movements in Andhra Pradesh: A Short History, in K. Murali Manohar, P. Ramaiah, and C. Sivaramakrishna Rao (eds.) *Political Economy of Tribal Development*, Indian Institute of Public Administration, Warangal, 1985.
123. Rao, Trinadha P. *Tribal Development in Question*, Laya Publications, Visakhapatnam, 2004.
124. Rao, Trinadha P. Nature of Opposition to Polavaram Project, *Economic and Political Weekly*, April 15, 2006.
125. Rao, Trinadha P. Persisting Alienation of Tribal Land, in Fr. Thomas Pallithanam (ed.), *Rekindling Hope, AP Social Watch Report*, Hyderabad, 2007.
126. Rao, Trinadha P. A status paper prepared for the 'Public Hearing on Community Forest Rights' organised by CFR

Learning and Advocacy group and Adivasi Janjati Adhikar Manch (AJAM) and other networks, at Constitution Club of India, New Delhi, 2013.

127. Ray, N. Introductory Address in K.S. Singh (ed.), *Tribal Situation in India*, IIAS, Shimla, 1972.
128. Reddy, Gopinath M., Anil Kumar K., Trinadha Rao P. and Oliver Springate Baginski. Obstructed Access to Forest Justice, The Implementation of Institutional Reform (FRA-2006) in *Andhra Pradesh Forested Landscapes*, CESS, Hyderabad, 2010.
129. Reddy, Prabhakar T. Tribal Land Alienation in Andhra Pradesh, *Economic and Political Weekly*, Vol. 24, No. 28, 1989, p. 1573.
130. Reddy, Subba N. Depriving Tribals of Land—Andhra Move to Amend Land Transfer Laws, *Economic and Political Weekly*, Vol. XXIII, No. 29, July 16, 1988, pp. 1458-61.
131. Reddy, Subba N. Sword of Damocles Over Tribal People of Andhra Pradesh, *Economic and Political Weekly*, July 1, 1989, pp. 1442-3.
132. Reddy, Subba N. Development Through Dismemberment of the Weak—Threat of Polavaram Project, *Economic and Political Weekly*, April 15, 2006, p. 1430-1.
133. *Report on Godavari Valley Girijana Ryotanga Porata Charita*, CPI(ML), 1997.
134 Roy, Burman B.K. *Communal Land System of the Tribals and Problems of Institutional Finance in Manipur and Tripura*, Delhi, 1986.
135. Roy, Burman J.J. Adivasi: A Contentious Term to Denote Tribes as Indigenous Peoples of India, *Mainstream*, Vol. XLVII, No. 32, 25 July 2009.
136. Samata Appellants vs. State of Andhra Pradesh & Others with Ms. Hyderabad Abrasives & Minerals (P) Ltd. (appellant) & State of Andhra Pradesh & Others, Respondents, AIR 1997 Supreme Court, p. 3297.
137. Sarapu Chinna Pothuraju Dora vs. District Collector, East Godavari District (2002 ALT 699).
138. Sardesai, G.S. *New History of the Marathas*, Bombay. Vol. II, 1948, p. 355.
139. Sastry, MSK. *Agency Laws in Andhra Pradesh*, ALT Publications, Hyderabad, 2011.
140. Sastry, V.N.V.K. *Between Gonds Rebellion*, Udyama Publications, Hyderabad, 1989.

141. Satyanarayana, K. *A Study of History and Culture of the Andhra*, People's Publishing House, New Delhi, 1975, p. 44.
142. Saxena, K.B. Tribal Land Alienation and Need for Policy Intervention, *The Administrator*, Vol. 34, 1991, pp. 89-98.
143. Saxena, K.B. Development as Destitution, *Alternative Economic Survey, India 2005–06: Disempowering Masses*, 2006.
144. Senapati, N. and Sahu, N.K. *Orissa District Gazetteers*, Koraput, O.G.P. 1966, pp. 70-1.
145. Shah, G. *Social Movements in India: A Review of Literature*, Sage, New Delhi, 1990.
146. Sharan, Ramesh. Alienation and Restoration of Tribal Land in Jharkhand – Current Issues and Possible Strategies, *Economic and Political Weekly*, October 8, 2005.
147. Sharma, T.R. Karl Marx: From Alienation to Exploitation, *Indian Journal of Political Science*, Vol. 40, No. 3 September 1979.
148. Singh, N. Emerging Problems of Ownership and Exploitation of Commercial Land in Tribal Society, *Man in India*, 1997.
149. Special Deputy Collector (TW), Rampachodavaram, E.G. District & others vs. Datla Venkapathi Raju & Others. 2003 (1) ALD 386 (D.B)) A similar view was taken by the court in G. Nageswararao @ China Nageswararao vs. Government of AP and Others.) 2007 (6) ALD 621.
150. Sub-Collector's Office, Land Records Register, Rampachoda-varam, E.G. District, 1986.
151. Sullivan to Chief Sec. September 9, 1879, Ibid; Joint Magistrate, Chodavaram, to District Magistrate, March 18, 1879, MJP, No. 313, March 25, 1879, in the Settlement of 1879-80, a small *chigurupannu* was incorporated in the *muttadars* 'kattubadi'.
152. Sundar, Nandini (ed.). *Legal Grounds*, Oxford University Press, New Delhi, 2009.
153. Sundaram, K. and Suresh Tendulkar. Poverty Among Social and Economic Groups in India in 1990s, *Economic and Political Weekly*, December 13, 2003.
154. *The Economist, A Spectre Haunting India*, August 17, 2006, see-online: <http://www.economist.com/world/asia/display story.cfm?story_id=7799247>.
154. Trivedi, H. *Tribal Land Systems: Land Reform Measures and Development of Tribals*, Concept Publishing Company, New Delhi, 1993.
155. UNDP. *Human Development Report 2004: Cultural Liberty in*

Today's Diverse World, Oxford University Press, New York, 2004.

156. Upadhyay, S. and Upadhyay V. *Handbook on Environmental Law, Vol. I: Forest Laws, Wildlife Laws and the Environment*, Lexis Nexis, Butterworths, New Delhi, 2002.
157. Vemana Somalamma & Another (Appl), Veera Sunkar Deo & Another (pet) vs. Deputy Collector (TW), Rampachodavaram, E.G. Dist, 1993(1) ALT 409 (F.B).
158. Vidyarthi, L.P. *The Maler: The Nature-Man-Spirit Complex in a Hill Tribe Introducing the Concept of 'Nature-Man-Spirit' in Anthropology* 1963 and Bharath Bhushan M. and Satyamohan, *P.V. Study of the Tribal Scenario in Andhra Pradesh*, 1990.
159. Viegas, Philip. *Encroached and Enslaved*, Indian Social Institute, New Delhi, 1991, p. 32.
160. Vuppuluri Veera Venkata Raju and Others vs. Special Deputy Tahsildar, Tribal Welfare, Gangavaram (V&M), E.G. District and Others. 2007 (6) ALD 292.
161. Vyas, N.N. Tribal Land Alienation: Recent Changes and New Dimensions, *Tribe*, Vol. 9, No. 3, 1975, p. 8
162. Xaxa, Virginius. Tribes as Indigenous People of India, *Economic and Political Weekly*, Vol. XXXIV, No. 51, December 18, 1999, pp. 3589-95.
163. Yunus, S.A. *Orissa, Land Alienation and Restoration on Tribal Communities in India*, S.N. Dubey and Ratan Murdia (eds.), Himalaya Publishing House, Bombay, 1979, p. 140.

Appendix 1

The Agency Tracts Interest and Land Transfer Act, 1917

(Act No. 1 of 1917) [August 14, 1917]

An Act to regulate, the rate of interest and the transfer of land in the Ganjam, Visakhapatnam and Godavari Agency Tracts.

Preamble: Whereas it is expedient to limit the rate of interest and to check transfers of land in the Agency Tracts of Ganjam, Visakhapatnam, and Godavari Districts:

It is hereby enacted as follows:

1. Short Title:
   This Act may be called the Agency Tracts Interest and Land Transfer Act, 1917.
2. Definition:
   In this Act unless there is anything repugnant in the subject or context—
   a. "Agency tracts" means the scheduled districts as defined in Acts XIV and XV of 1847 and included within the districts of Ganjam, Visakhapatnam and Godavari.
   b. "Agent" means "Agent to the Governor" in the districts of Ganjam and Visakhapatnam and "Government Agent" in the district of Godavari.
   c. "Hill tribe" means any body or class of persons resident in the Agency tracts (not being a landholder as defined in [the Andhra Pradesh (Andhra Area) Estates Land Act, 1908 (Act 1 of 1908) that may form time to time be notified as such for the purposes of the Act by the [State Government].

d. "Immovable Property" does not include standing timber, growing crops or grass.
e. "Prescribed" means prescribed by rules made under this Act.
f. "Transfer" means mortgage with or without possession, lease, gift, exchange or any other dealing with property not being a testamentary disposition and includes a charge or any contract relating to immovable property.

3. Maximum interest that may be allowed as against a member of a hill tribe:

   In any suit instituted after the commencement of this Act, notwithstanding any agreement to the contrary, —

   a. Interest on any debt or liability shall not as against a member of a hill tribe allowed or decreed at a higher rate than twenty-four per centum per annum nor shall any compound interest or any collateral advantage be allowed as against him.
   b. The total interest allowed or decreed on any debt or liability as against a member of a hill tribe shall not exceed the principal amount.

4. Transfer of immovable property by a member of a hill tribe:

   a. Notwithstanding any rule of law or enactment to the contrary, any transfer of immovable property situated within the Agency tracts by a member of a hill tribe shall be absolutely null and void unless made in favour of another member of a hill tribe, or with the previous consent in writing of the Agent or of any other prescribed officer.
   b. Where a transfer of property is made in contravention of sub-section(1), the Agent or any other prescribed officer may, on application by any one interested, decree Ejectment against any person in possession of the property claiming under the transfer and may restore it to the transferor or his heirs.
   c. Subject to such conditions as may be prescribed an appeal against a decree or order under sub-section(2) if made by the Agent shall lie to the State Government and if made by any other officer shall lie to the Assistant Agent or to the Agent as may be prescribed.

5. Suits against a member of a hill tribe to be instituted in the Agency Courts:
   Notwithstanding the provisions of any law to the contrary, every suit against a member of a hill tribe instituted after the commencement of this Act shall be instituted only in the Courts of the Agency tracts.
6. Attachment of immovable property:
   In execution of a money-decree against a member of a hill tribe, no immovable property owned by him within the Agency tracts shall be liable to be attached and sold except as and if prescribed.
7. Farming of rules:
   a. The State Government may from time to time make rules to carry out the purposes of the Act.
   b. All rules made under this section shall be published in the [Official Gazette] and, on such publication, shall have the same effects if enacted in this Act.
8. Savings:
   a. This Act shall not affect transfer made or debts or liabilities incurred before the coming into force of this Act.
   b. Nothing in this Act shall affect a landholder's right to proceed against the *ryot* in accordance with the provisions of the [Andhra Pradesh (Andhra Area) Estates Land Act, 1908 (Act 1 of 1908)] or the first charge declared by Section 5 of that Act, or the provisions of the said Act regarding relinquishment of a holding by a *ryot*.

Appendix 2

The Andhra Pradesh Scheduled Areas Land Transfer Regulation, 1959

(Regulation No. 1 of 1959)
[March 4, 1959]

A Regulation to regulate the transfer of land in the Scheduled Areas of the East Godavari, West Godavari, Visakhapatnam, Srikakulam [Adilabad, Warangal, Khammam and Mahaboobnagar] districts of Andhra Pradesh.

Be it enacted in the Tenth Year of the Republic of India as follows:

1. Short title and commencement:
   a) This Regulation may be called the Andhra Pradesh Scheduled Areas Land Transfer Regulation, 1959.
   b) It shall come into force at once.
2. Definitions:
   In this Regulation, unless the context otherwise requires:
   a) 'Agency tracts' means the Areas in the districts of East Godavari, West Godavari, Visakhapatnam, Srikakulam, [Adilabad, Warangal, Khammam and Mahaboobnagar] declared from time to time as Scheduled Areas by the President under sub-paragraph(1) of paragraph 6 of the Fifth Schedule to the Constitution.
   b) "Agent" means the person designated by the State Government as an "Agent to the Government" in the districts of East Godavari, West Godavari, Visakhapatnam, Srikakulam, Adilabad, Warangal, Khammam and Mahaboobnagar as the case may be.
   c) "Agency Divisional Officer" means the person designated

by the State Government as "Agency Divisional Officer" for the purpose of this Regulation;

d) 'Immovable property' includes standing crops, timber and trees, but does not include growing grass.

e) 'Prescribed' means prescribed in rules made under this regulation.

f) 'Scheduled Tribe' means any tribe or tribal community or part of or group within any tribe or tribal community and specified as such in relation to the State of Andhra Pradesh by public notification by the President under clause(1) of Article 342 of the Constitution'.

Clause (f) is substituted as per the Andhra Pradesh Scheduled Areas Land Transfer (Amendment) Regulation, 1978*.

g) 'Transfer' means mortgage with or without possession lease, sale, gift, exchange or any other dealing with immovable property, not being a testamentary disposition and includes a charge on such property or a contract relating to such property in respect of such mortgage, lease, sale, gift, exchange or other dealing.

3. Transfer of immovable property by a member of a Schedule Tribe:

1) a. Notwithstanding anything in any enactment, rule or law in force in the Agency tracts any transfer of immovable property situated in the Agency tracts by a person. Whether or not such a person is a member of a Scheduled Tribe, shall be absolutely null and void, unless such transfer is made in favour of a person, who is a member of a Scheduled Tribe or a society registered or deemed to be registered under the Andhra Pradesh Cooperative Societies Act, 1964 (Act 7 of 1964) which composed solely of members of the Scheduled Tribes.

b. Until the contrary is proved, any immovable property situated in the Agency tracts and in the possession of a person who is not a member of Scheduled Tribe, shall be presumed to have been acquired by the person or his predecessor in possession through a transfer or his predecessor in possession through a transfer made to him by a member of a Scheduled Tribe.

c. Where a person intending to sell his land is not able to effect such a sale, by reason of the fact that no member of a Scheduled Tribe is willing to purchase the land or is willing to purchase the land on the terms offered by such a person, then such a person may apply to the Agent, the Agency Divisional Officer or any other prescribed officer for the acquisition of such land by the State Government, and the Agent. The Agency Divisional Officer or the prescribed officer, as the case may by order, take over such land on payment of compensation in accordance with the principles specified in Section 10 of the Andhra Pradesh Ceiling on Agricultural Holdings Act, 1961 (Act X of 1961), and such land shall there upon vest in the State Government free from all encumbrances and shall be disposed of in favour of members of the Scheduled Tribes or a society registered or deemed to be registered under the Andhra Pradesh Co-operative Societies Act, 1964 (Act 7 of 1964) composed solely of members of the Scheduled Tribes or in such other manner and subject to such conditions as may be prescribed];

1) a. Where a Transfer of immovable property is made in contravention of sub-section (1), the Agent, the Agency Divisional Officer or any other prescribed Officer may, on application by any one interested, or on information given in writing by a public servant, or *suo motu* decree ejectment against any person in possession of the property claiming under the transfer, after due notice to him in the manner prescribed and may restore it to the transfer or his heirs.

b. If the Transferor or his heirs are not willing to take back the property or where their whereabouts are not known, the Agent, the Agency Divisional Officer or prescribed officer, as the case may be, may order the assignment or sale of the property to any other member of a Scheduled Tribe [or a society registered or deemed to be registered under any law relating to Cooperative Societies for the time being in force in the State] composed solely of members of the Scheduled Tribes, or otherwise dispose of it, as if it was a property at the disposal of the State Government.

2 a. Subject to such conditions as may be prescribed, an appeal against any decree or order under sub-section (2), shall lie within such times as may be prescribed –

i. If the decree or order was passed by the Agent, to the State Government.

ii If the decree or order was passed by the Agency Divisional Officer, to the Agent; and

iii If the decree or order was passed by any other officer, to the Agency Divisional Officer or Agent, as may be prescribed.

a. The appellate authority may entertain an appeal on sufficient cause being shown after the expiry of the time limit prescribed therefore.

[4 For the purpose of this section, the expression 'transfer' includes a sale in execution of decree and also a transfer made by a member of a Scheduled Tribe in favour of any other member of a Scheduled Tribe *benami* for the benefit of a person who is not a member of a Scheduled Tribe; but does not include a partition or a devolution by succession.]

3A. Special provision in respect of mortgages without possession: Notwithstanding anything contained in this Regulation or in any enactment, rule or law in force in the Agency Tracts,—

1. Any person, whether or not such person is member of a Schedule Tribe, may, subject to the provisions of Clause (2) mortgage without possession, any immovable property situated in the Agency tracts, to any Cooperative Society including a land mortgage bank, or to any 1 [XXX] bank or other financial institution approved by the State Government.

Explanation

For the purpose of this clause, 'a bank' means a banking company as detained in Clause(c) of Section 5 of the Banking Regulation Act, 1949 and includes the State Bank of India constituted under the State Bank of India Act, 1955, a subsidiary bank as defined in the State Bank of India (Subsidiary Banks) Act, 1959, a corresponding a new bank as specified in the First Schedule to the Banking Companies

(Acquisition and Transfer of Undertakings) Act, 1970, the Agricultural Refinance and Development Corporation established under the Agricultural Refinance and development Corporation Act, 1963, a Regional Rural Bank established under the Regional Rural Banks Act, 1976, and any other banking institution notified by the Central Government under Section 51 of the Banking Regulation Act, 1949.

2 In respect of every mortgage which was executed at any time either before or after the date of commencement of the Andhra Pradesh Scheduled Areas Land Transfer (Amendment) Regulation, 1971, in the event of the immovable property so mortgaged or any part thereof being brought to sale in default of payment of the mortgage money or the interest thereof or for any other purpose, the said property shall be sold only to a member of a Scheduled Tribe or society registered or deemed to be registered under the Andhra Pradesh Cooperative Societies Act, 1954 (Act 7 of 1954) which is composed solely of members of the Scheduled Tribes.

Explanation

For the purpose of Section 3-B and this section a Cooperative Society having as its members all or any of the following, namely:

a. The individual members of the Scheduled Tribes;
b. One or more cooperative societies which does not have among its members any person who is not a member of a Scheduled Tribe;
c. The Government shall be deemed to be a society registered or deemed to be registered under the Andhra Pradesh Co-operative Societies Act, 1964 (Act 7 of 1964) which is composed solely of members of the Scheduled Tribes.

3 B. Restriction on registration of documents:

Notwithstanding anything contained in the Registration Act, 1908, no document relating to transfer of immovable property situated in the agency tracts shall be registered by any person situated in the agency tracts shall be registered by any registering officer appointed under the said Act, unless the person presenting the document furnished a declaration by the transferee in the prescribed form which shall be subject to verification in the prescribed manner that the transferee is a member of a Scheduled Tribe or a society registered or deemed to be registered under the Andhra Pradesh Co-operative Societies Act, 1964 which is composed solely of members of the Scheduled Tribes'.

4. Suits against a member of a Scheduled Tribe to be instituted in the Agency Courts:
   Notwithstanding anything contained in any enactment, rule or law in force in the Agency tracts, every suit against a member of a Scheduled Tribe instituted after the commencement of this Regulation shall be instituted only in the Court having jurisdiction over the Agency tracts.
5. Attachment and sale of immovable property:
   No immovable property situated in the Agency tracts and owned by a member of a Scheduled Tribe shall be able to be attached and sold in execution of a money decree against such member, except to the extent and the manner prescribed.
6. Revision:
   The State Government may revise any decree of order passed by the Agent, the Agency Divisional Officer or any other prescribed officer under this Regulation.
   Provided that this power shall be exercised only after due notice to the parties affected by the decree of order and after giving them a reasonable opportunity of being heard.

6-A. Penalty:

1. Any person who, on or after the commencement of the Andhra Pradesh Scheduled Areas Land Transfer (Amended) Regulation, 1978.
   a. Acquires any immovable property in convention of the provisions of this Regulation; or
   b. Continues in possession of such property after a decree for ejectment is passed;

   Shall on conviction be punished with rigorous imprisonment for a term which may extend to one year or with fine which may extend to Rs. 2000 or with both.
2. When a Court imposes a sentence of fine or a sentence of which fine forms a part, the Court may, when passing a

judgement, order any part of the fine recovered to be paid to the member of a Scheduled Tribe who is a transferor, as compensation.

7. Provisions of Limitation Act to apply to proceedings under this Regulation:
   The provisions of the Indian Limitation Act, 1908 (Central Act IX of 1908), shall, in so far as they are not inconsistent with the provisions of this Regulation or the rules made there under, apply to proceedings under this Regulation.
8. **Power to make rules:**
   1. The State Government may, from time to make rules to carry out the purposes of this Regulation.
   2. All rules made under this section shall be published in the Andhra Pradesh Gazette and on such publication shall have the same effect as if enacted in this Regulation.
9. Repeal:

   The Agency Tract Interest and Land Transfer Act, 1917 (Madras Act of 1 of 1917) is hereby repealed to the extent to which any of the provisions contained therein correspond or are repugnant, to any of the provisions contained in this Regulation.
10. Savings:

    1 The provisions contained in this Regulation shall not affect:
      a. Any transfer made or sale effected in execution of a decree of before the commencement of the Agency Tracts Interest and Land Transfer Act, 1917(Madras Act 1 of 1917); or
      b. Any transfer made or sale effected in execution of a decree after the commencement of the said Act and before the commencement of this Regulation, if such a transfer or sale was valid under the provisions of the said Act.

    2 Nothing in this Regulation shall affect a land-holder's right to proceed against a *ryot* in accordance with the provisions of the Andhra Pradesh (Andhra area) Estates Land Act, 1908 (Act 1 of 1908) or the first charge declared by Section

5 of the Act or the provisions of that Act regarding relinquishment of the holding by a *ryot* or the provisions of the Central Provincial Tenancy Act, 1898 (Central Act IX of 1898);

Provided that no relinquishment of a holding by a *ryot* who is a member of a Scheduled Tribe shall be valid unless the previous sanction of the State Government, or subject to the rules made in this behalf the previous consent in writing of the Agent or the prescribed Officer, has been obtained thereto.